127th Edition

Travel to Grand Rapids Michigan

2023
People Who Know
Publishing
Jack Ross

Forward: In this book, People Who Know Publishing will provide a travel guide of 101+ things to see, do and visit in Grand Rapids Michigan. We strive to make our guides as comprehensive and complete as possible. We publish travel guides on cities and countries all over the world. Feel free to check out our complete list of travel guides here:

People Who Know Publishing partners with local experts to produce travel guides on various locations. We differentiate ourselves from other travel books by focusing on areas not typically covered by others. Our guides include a detailed history of the location and its population. In addition to covering all of the "must see" areas of a location such as museums and local sights, we also provide up-to-date restaurant suggestions and local food traditions.

To make a request for a travel guide on a particular area or to join our email list to stay updated on travel tips from local experts sign up here: https://mailchi.mp/c74b62620b1f/travel-books

Be sure to confirm restaurants, addresses, and phone numbers as those may have changed since the book was published.

About the Author:

Jack Ross is a college student who was born in Westchester County, NY. He's an expert on the local "in the know" tips of the area and is an authority on Westchester and its towns. He's been featured in several publications including Business Insider and CNBC for his books.

During his spare time, he writes, plays tennis and golf and enjoys all water sports (including his latest favorite, the eFoil). Jack also enjoys traveling and is a food connoisseur throughout Westchester. Jack travels consistently and has been to majority of the states in the U.S.

Sign up for our email list to get inside access to the towns and places we cover!
>> https://mailchi.mp/c74b62620b1f/travel-books
>> https://mailchi.mp/c74b62620b1f/travel-books

Table of Contents

Grand Rapids Michigan

State: Michigan
Population: 198,893
Ranking in U.S.: N/A
County: Kent County
Founded: 1826
Tag line: N/A

Introduction

"There's a unique blend of art, culture, and history in Grand Rapids that sets it apart." - Unknown

Nestled along the banks of the Grand River, Grand Rapids stands as a dynamic and culturally rich city in the heart of West Michigan. Known for its friendly community, thriving arts scene, and diverse recreational opportunities, Grand Rapids has earned its reputation as a hidden gem in the Midwest. This city seamlessly blends urban sophistication with natural beauty, offering residents and visitors a unique and engaging experience.

Grand Rapids has become a hub for creativity and innovation, most notably through events like ArtPrize, an international art competition that transforms the city into an open canvas for artists worldwide. The city's commitment to the arts is further reflected in its numerous galleries, theaters, and public installations.

Beyond its artistic allure, Grand Rapids proudly carries the title of "Beer City, USA," with a burgeoning craft beer scene that has garnered national acclaim. The city's breweries not only produce exceptional beers but also contribute to the lively and convivial atmosphere that defines Grand Rapids.

Nature enthusiasts can explore the city's well-maintained parks, picturesque trails, and the scenic riverfront, providing a welcome respite from urban life. The Grand River, which winds through the heart of the city, adds both charm and recreational opportunities, making it a central feature of Grand Rapids' landscape.

With a strong sense of community pride, a commitment to sustainability, and a welcoming spirit, Grand Rapids invites visitors to discover its unique blend of cultural sophistication, natural beauty, and Midwestern warmth. Whether strolling through art-filled streets, savoring local flavors, or enjoying the outdoors, Grand Rapids offers a diverse and memorable experience for all who explore its vibrant neighborhoods and inviting spaces.

History

Native Inhabitants:
Before European contact, the region was inhabited by various Native American tribes, including the Ottawa, Potawatomi, and Ojibwe. The Grand River Valley was a vital area for trade and transportation.

European Exploration and Settlement:
The first European to explore the Grand Rapids area was French explorer Louis Campau in the late 18th century. The fur trade became a significant economic activity, attracting European settlers.

Founding and Growth:
In 1826, Campau officially established the trading post and village of Grand Rapids. The settlement grew due to its strategic location along the Grand River and the availability of natural resources.

Timber and Furniture Industry:
In the mid-19th century, Grand Rapids became known for its booming timber industry. The abundant forests facilitated the growth of lumber mills, and the city earned the nickname "Furniture City" due to its prominence in the production of fine furniture.

Economic Expansion:
With the completion of the Grand Rapids and
Indiana Railroad in the 1860s, the city's economy
further expanded, enabling easier transportation of
goods and materials.

Urban Renewal and Economic Challenges:
Like many American cities, Grand Rapids faced
challenges in the mid-20th century, including urban
decay and economic struggles. However, the city
underwent a revitalization process in subsequent
decades, focusing on downtown development and
cultural initiatives.

Art and Culture Renaissance:
The late 20th century and early 21st century saw a
cultural renaissance in Grand Rapids. Events like
ArtPrize, an international art competition, drew
attention to the city's artistic vibrancy.

Economic Diversity:
Grand Rapids has diversified its economy beyond
manufacturing and furniture production. Health care,
technology, and education sectors have become significant
contributors to the city's prosperity.

Economy

1. Diversified Economy:
Grand Rapids has successfully diversified its economy over the years. While historically known for furniture manufacturing, the city now boasts a broad economic base, including sectors like healthcare, technology, education, and services.

2. Healthcare and Medical Research:
The healthcare sector plays a significant role in Grand Rapids' economy. The city is home to several major hospitals, medical research institutions, and healthcare-related businesses.

3. Manufacturing:
Although the prominence of furniture manufacturing has decreased compared to the past, manufacturing remains a vital component of Grand Rapids' economy. The city continues to be involved in various manufacturing activities, contributing to its economic stability.

4. Technology and Innovation:
Grand Rapids has seen growth in the technology and innovation sectors. The city has supported initiatives to foster a culture of entrepreneurship and innovation, attracting tech companies and startups.

5. Education and Research:
The presence of educational institutions, including Grand Valley State University and others, contributes to the education sector's role in the local economy. Research activities and partnerships with industries also enhance the city's economic landscape.

6. Small Business and Entrepreneurship:
Grand Rapids has a thriving community of small businesses and entrepreneurs. The city supports local initiatives that promote small business growth and sustainability.

Transportation Systems

1. Public Transit:

The Rapid: The public transit system in Grand Rapids is operated by The Rapid, which provides bus services throughout the city and surrounding areas. The Rapid offers various routes, including those serving downtown, residential neighborhoods, and commercial areas.

2. Personal Vehicles:

Like many American cities, personal vehicles are a common mode of transportation in Grand Rapids. The city is well-connected by roads and highways, facilitating easy travel by car.

3. Bicycling:

Grand Rapids has been working to become more bike-friendly, with dedicated bike lanes and trails. The city's efforts to promote cycling as a mode of transportation and recreation include the development of bike-sharing programs and initiatives to enhance bike infrastructure.

4. Walking:

Downtown Grand Rapids is pedestrian-friendly, with sidewalks and pedestrian-friendly areas. Many residents and visitors find walking to be a convenient way to explore the city center.

5. Ride-Sharing Services:

Ride-sharing services such as Uber and Lyft operate in Grand Rapids, providing additional transportation options for those who prefer on-demand, private car services.

6. Gerald R. Ford International Airport:

The Gerald R. Ford International Airport serves as the primary airport for Grand Rapids and the surrounding region. It provides domestic and limited international flights, connecting the city to various destinations.

Neighborhoods

Heritage Hill:
Known for its historic charm, Heritage Hill is a residential neighborhood featuring 19th and early 20th-century homes. It's one of the largest urban historic districts in the United States.

Eastown:
Eastown is a vibrant and eclectic neighborhood known for its local shops, restaurants, and a bohemian atmosphere. It's a popular area for young professionals and artists.

Downtown:
The heart of the city, Downtown Grand Rapids, is a bustling area with a mix of businesses, entertainment venues, and cultural attractions. It includes areas like Heartside and Monroe Center.

Cherry Hill:
Cherry Hill is a historic neighborhood located southwest of downtown. It features a mix of residential homes and commercial spaces, and it's known for its architectural diversity.

Creston:
Creston is a neighborhood in the northern part of the city. It has a mix of residential and commercial areas and is known for its community events and local businesses.

Garfield Park:
Situated south of downtown, Garfield Park is a residential neighborhood with a large park of the same name. The park offers recreational amenities and green spaces.

Food

Michigan Craft Beer:
Grand Rapids has earned the title of "Beer City, USA," and it's renowned for its thriving craft beer scene. With numerous breweries and taprooms, you can explore a variety of locally brewed beers, including IPAs, stouts, and unique seasonal offerings.

Farm-to-Table Cuisine:
The city embraces the farm-to-table movement, and many restaurants in Grand Rapids prioritize locally sourced, fresh ingredients. You can enjoy dishes that highlight the flavors of the region's agricultural products.

Cider and Donuts:
Michigan is known for its apple orchards, and in the fall, cider mills become popular destinations. Enjoy freshly pressed apple cider paired with warm cinnamon sugar donuts for a delicious and quintessential Michigan treat.

Vernors Ginger Ale:
Vernors, a popular ginger ale brand, originated in Michigan. While not a food item, trying this regional beverage is a unique and refreshing experience.

Pasties:
Pasties, a traditional Cornish pastry filled with meat, potatoes, and vegetables, have found a place in the culinary scene in Grand Rapids. They make for a hearty and comforting meal.

Dutch Influence:
Grand Rapids has a strong Dutch heritage, and you can find Dutch-inspired treats like stroopwafels and poffertjes in local bakeries. Additionally, the city hosts an annual Tulip Time Festival, celebrating Dutch culture.

Here are our ten favorite restaurant recommendations!

The Grove:
A farm-to-table restaurant with a focus on seasonal and locally sourced ingredients. The menu features creative dishes in a stylish and inviting atmosphere.

Maru Sushi & Grill:
Known for its fresh and inventive sushi offerings, Maru Sushi & Grill combines traditional Japanese flavors with modern twists. The restaurant has a sleek and contemporary ambiance.

Terra GR:
A farm-to-table eatery with an emphasis on sustainability. Terra GR offers a diverse menu with options for various dietary preferences, including vegetarian and gluten-free.

Founders Brewing Co. - Grand Rapids:
While primarily known as a brewery, Founders Brewing Co. also has a taproom that serves excellent food. The menu complements their craft beer selection with items like sandwiches, burgers, and barbecue.

Leo's Restaurant:
Leo's is a seafood and steakhouse with an upscale ambiance. It's known for its fresh seafood selections, oyster bar, and classic steakhouse offerings.

Donkey Taqueria:
A popular spot for Mexican cuisine, Donkey Taqueria offers a casual and lively atmosphere. Tacos, street corn, and margaritas are among the favorites.

The Green Well Gastro Pub:
A gastropub committed to using local and sustainable ingredients. The menu features a range of comfort food and pub classics with a modern twist.

Osteria Rossa:
A contemporary Italian restaurant offering a variety of pasta dishes, wood-fired pizzas, and Italian-inspired entrees. The atmosphere is warm and inviting.

Butcher's Union:
A gastropub with a focus on craft cocktails and a menu that includes a variety of meats, sandwiches, and shareable plates. The ambiance is rustic and cozy.

The Electric Cheetah:
Known for its eclectic and creative menu, The Electric Cheetah serves a variety of comfort food, including burgers, macaroni and cheese, and unique desserts. The restaurant has a funky and vibrant atmosphere.

Nightlife

Founders Brewing Co.:
Known for its craft beer, Founders Brewing Co. is not only a popular brewery but also a lively spot with a spacious taproom. They often host live music events, and the atmosphere is casual and vibrant.

The Pyramid Scheme:
A versatile venue hosting live music, comedy shows, and dance parties. The Pyramid Scheme is known for its diverse events, including concerts featuring local and touring bands.

Stella's Lounge:
A retro-style bar with a vast selection of craft beers and creative cocktails. Stella's Lounge also offers classic arcade games and is known for its laid-back and quirky atmosphere.

Mojo's Dueling Piano Bar:
For a fun and interactive night out, Mojo's Dueling Piano Bar is a popular choice. Talented pianists take requests and perform in a high-energy, entertaining atmosphere.

Billy's Lounge:
A longtime staple of the Grand Rapids music scene, Billy's Lounge features live bands, dance nights, and themed events. The venue has a relaxed vibe and is a favorite among locals.

Local Traditions & Customs

Art and Culture Celebrations:
Grand Rapids celebrates its vibrant arts scene through events like ArtPrize, an international art competition that transforms the city into an open gallery. The competition invites artists from around the world to display their work in public spaces, engaging the community in the appreciation of art.

Tulip Time Festival:
Grand Rapids, with its strong Dutch heritage, hosts the annual Tulip Time Festival. This springtime event features traditional Dutch dance performances, parades, and the blooming of thousands of tulips. It pays homage to the city's Dutch roots and attracts visitors from near and far.

Beer Culture:
As "Beer City, USA," Grand Rapids has a robust craft beer culture. Local breweries, beer festivals, and a community appreciation for craft beverages contribute to a beer-centric lifestyle. Residents often participate in brewery tours and beer-related events.

Outdoor Recreation:
Grand Rapids' proximity to natural resources, including the Grand River and various parks, promotes outdoor activities. Residents often engage in hiking, biking, kayaking, and other outdoor pursuits. There's a sense of community around enjoying the natural beauty of the region.

Local Food Movement:
Grand Rapids has embraced the local food movement, with an emphasis on farm-to-table dining. Farmers' markets, community-supported agriculture (CSA), and restaurants sourcing locally grown produce contribute to a culture of sustainable and locally sourced food.

What to buy?

Local Art and Crafts:
Explore local art galleries and craft markets to find unique pieces created by Grand Rapids artists. This could include paintings, sculptures, pottery, and other handmade crafts.

Craft Beer and Brewery Merchandise:
Given its status as "Beer City, USA," you can find a wide range of craft beers produced by local breweries. Consider picking up a selection of craft beers or brewery merchandise such as branded glassware, shirts, or coasters.

Dutch-inspired Items:
Grand Rapids has Dutch heritage, so you might find Dutch-inspired items like wooden clogs, Delftware, or tulip-themed souvenirs. Visit local shops or markets that celebrate the city's Dutch roots.

Local Food Products:
Explore local farmers' markets or specialty food stores for unique food products. Look for Michigan-made jams, honey, maple syrup, cherry products, or other locally sourced items.

Grand Rapids-themed Apparel:
Many local shops offer clothing and accessories that showcase Grand Rapids pride. T-shirts, hoodies, hats, or other apparel featuring the city's name or landmarks make for great souvenirs.

Books by Local Authors:
Visit local bookstores to discover works by authors from the Grand Rapids area or books that showcase the city's history and culture.

Finally, here are the five most famous people from the city!

Gerald Ford, the 38th President of the United States, was born in Omaha, Nebraska, but spent much of his childhood in Grand Rapids. His childhood home is now part of the Gerald R. Ford Presidential Museum.

Betsy DeVos, a businesswoman and former Secretary of Education under President Donald Trump, has strong ties to Grand Rapids. She is known for her philanthropy and advocacy for education reform.

Floyd Mayweather Jr.:
While born in Grand Rapids, Floyd Mayweather Jr., one of the greatest boxers of all time, spent much of his early life there. Mayweather has an undefeated professional record and is considered one of the most successful and wealthy athletes in the world.

Roger B. Chaffee, an astronaut, was born in Grand Rapids. He was one of the astronauts chosen for the Apollo program but tragically lost his life in the Apollo 1 spacecraft fire during a pre-launch test.

Lucius Lyon was a U.S. Senator from Michigan and played a significant role in the early development of Grand Rapids. Lyon Street in Grand Rapids is named after him.

101+ things to do in the city

1. Explore the Gerald R. Ford Presidential Museum.
2. Attend an ArtPrize event.
3. Take a stroll through the Frederik Meijer Gardens & Sculpture Park.
4. Visit the Grand Rapids Art Museum.
5. Attend a live performance at the DeVos Performance Hall.
6. Explore the historic Heritage Hill neighborhood.
7. Walk along the Grand River Heritage Trail.
8. Visit the Grand Rapids Public Museum.
9. Attend a concert or event at Van Andel Arena.
10. Experience the John Ball Zoo.
11. Take a scenic drive along the M-22 route.
12. Attend a game or event at Fifth Third Ballpark.
13. Explore local breweries on the Beer City Ale Trail.
14. Visit the Grand Rapids Children's Museum.
15. Go hiking at Millennium Park.
16. Attend the Tulip Time Festival in Holland (near Grand Rapids).
17. Explore the Medical Mile district.
18. Attend a Broadway Grand Rapids performance.
19. Enjoy a picnic at Riverside Park.
20. Explore the Fulton Street Farmers Market.
21. Visit the UICA (Urban Institute for Contemporary Arts).
22. Go kayaking on the Grand River.
23. Attend a performance at the Actors' Theatre Grand Rapids.
24. Take a brewery tour at Founders Brewing Co.
25. Go ice skating at Rosa Parks Circle in winter.
26. Attend a concert at the Intersection.
27. Explore the trails at Blandford Nature Center.
28. Visit the Grand Rapids African American Museum & Archives.
29. Attend the Festival of the Arts.
30. Explore the Eastown neighborhood.
31. Visit the Grand Rapids Civic Theatre.
32. Attend the Hispanic Festival.
33. Take a scenic drive through Fallasburg Park.
34. Explore the Gaslight Village in East Grand Rapids.
35. Attend a comedy show at Dr. Grins Comedy Club.
36. Take a horse-drawn carriage ride downtown.
37. Explore the sculptures along the Grand Rapids African American Memorial Trail.
38. Attend a Grand Rapids Symphony performance.
39. Take a walk or bike ride along the White Pine Trail.
40. Visit the Voigt House Victorian Museum.

41.Explore local shops in the East Hills neighborhood.

42.Attend the Polish Festival.

43.Take a day trip to Lake Michigan's beaches.

44.Visit the Gerald R. Ford Boyhood Home.

45.Explore the West Side neighborhood.

46.Go fishing at the Rogue River.

47.Attend a poetry reading at the Literary Life Bookstore & More.

48.Explore the Creston neighborhood.

49.Take a scenic drive through the Fruit Ridge.

50.Attend a performance at Circle Theatre.

51.Explore the Alger Heights neighborhood.

52.Attend the Festival of the Arts.

53.Visit the Van Andel Museum Center at the Public Museum.

54.Attend a workshop or class at the Grand Rapids Art Center.

55.Go mountain biking at Merrell Trail.

56.Attend the Asian-Pacific Festival.

57.Explore the John Ball Park Zoo Wildlife Conservation Center.

58.Take a walk around Reed's Lake in East Grand Rapids.

59.Visit the Grand Rapids African American Health Institute.

60.Attend the Grand Rapids Balloon Festival.

61.Explore the Alpine Avenue shopping district.

62.Attend the Diwali Festival of Lights.

63.Visit the Grand Rapids Public Library.

64.Attend a River City Improv show.

65. Explore the Roosevelt Park neighborhood.

66.Go birdwatching at Aman Park.

67.Attend a lecture or event at Grand Valley State University.

68.Explore the West Michigan Whitecaps stadium.

69.Attend the West Michigan Pet Expo.

70.Explore the Belknap Lookout neighborhood.

71.Go rollerblading at Richmond Park.

72.Attend the Polish Heritage Society Annual Dozynki Festival.

73.Explore the West Grand neighborhood.

74.Attend the Latinx Art Exhibition.

75.Visit the Friends of Grand Rapids Parks.

76.Explore the Midtown neighborhood.

77.Go horseback riding at Kent Trails.

78.Attend the Taste of Grand Rapids.

79.Explore the Michigan Street Medical Mile.

80.Attend the Lantern Launch at Robinette's Apple Haus & Winery.

81.Go rock climbing at Higher Ground Rock Climbing Centre.

82.Attend the Grand Rapids Asian-Pacific Festival.
83.Explore the Madison Square neighborhood.
84.Go zip-lining at Cannonsburg Ski Area.
85.Attend the GRandJazzFest.
86.Explore the Oakdale neighborhood.
87.Go paddleboarding on Reeds Lake.
88.Attend the West Michigan Chalk Art Festival.
89.Explore the Ottawa Hills neighborhood.
90.Go snowshoeing at Provin Trails Park.
91.Attend the International Wine, Beer & Food Festival.
92.Explore the Garfield Park neighborhood.
93.Attend the Grand Rapids Film Festival.
94.Go cross-country skiing at Pigeon Creek Park.
95 Attend a beer or wine tasting event.
96.Attend the Local First Street Party.
97.Go geocaching in local parks.
98.Attend the GR Hiking & Yoga Meetup events.
99.Explore the Cheshire Village neighborhood.
100.Go disc golfing at Johnson Park.
101.Attend the Downtown Market Grand Rapids events.
102.Explore the Beckwith Hills neighborhood.
103.Go fishing at Reed's Lake in East Grand Rapids.
104.Attend a cooking class at the Downtown Market Grand Rapids.
105.Explore the Mulick Park neighborhood.
106.Go tubing or sledding at Cannonsburg Ski Area.
107.Attend the Gerald R. Ford Memorial Day Parade.
108.Explore the Shawmut Hills neighborhood.
109.Go camping at PJ Hoffmaster State Park.
110.Attend the Polish Heritage Festival.

1.Explore the Gerald R. Ford Presidential Museum.

Exploring the Gerald R. Ford Presidential Museum in Grand Rapids is a captivating and enriching experience that delves into the life and political career of the 38th President of the United States. Nestled along the picturesque Grand River, the museum not only serves as a tribute to Gerald Ford but also as a comprehensive historical archive. Visitors are treated to a journey through Ford's early years in Grand Rapids, offering insights into the formative experiences that shaped his character and leadership style.

As you navigate the museum, you'll encounter a diverse array of exhibits that chronicle Ford's tenure in office during a pivotal period in American history. From his unexpected ascent to the presidency following the resignation of Richard Nixon to his efforts in healing a nation grappling with the aftermath of Watergate, the displays showcase the challenges and triumphs of Ford's presidency. Artifacts, documents, and multimedia presentations provide a nuanced perspective on his decision-making processes and the impact of his policies.

The museum's commitment to historical accuracy and educational engagement ensures that visitors gain a comprehensive understanding of Ford's role in shaping the trajectory of the United States during a critical era. The scenic location along the river adds an extra layer of ambiance, allowing visitors to reflect on the historical significance of the exhibits while enjoying picturesque views.

Overall, a visit to the Gerald R. Ford Presidential Museum is not just a walk through history; it's an immersive exploration that invites contemplation, discussion, and a deeper appreciation for the complexities of leadership and governance. Whether you're a history enthusiast, a student of political science, or simply curious about the nation's past, this museum offers a compelling narrative that transcends time and resonates with the ongoing evolution of American democracy.

2.Attend an ArtPrize event.

Attending an ArtPrize event in Grand Rapids is an immersive and dynamic experience that celebrates the intersection of art, community, and creativity.

ArtPrize, a unique and open international art competition, transforms the city into a vibrant canvas where artists from around the world showcase their talent in diverse mediums and styles. The event typically takes place across numerous venues, turning museums, galleries, parks, and even public spaces into exhibition sites for a wide range of artistic expressions.

As you explore ArtPrize, you'll encounter thought-provoking sculptures, paintings, installations, and interactive pieces that captivate the imagination. The decentralized nature of the event encourages attendees to meander through the city, discovering hidden gems and engaging with artists in an informal and accessible setting. The diversity of artistic perspectives and the sheer scale of the exhibition create a unique atmosphere, fostering conversations about art and its impact on society.

One of the distinctive features of ArtPrize is its open voting system, allowing visitors to actively participate in the selection of winners. This democratic approach not only encourages public engagement but also reflects the inclusive spirit of the event. The city comes alive with energy as locals and visitors alike immerse themselves in the art, contributing to a sense of shared cultural celebration.

ArtPrize is not just an event; it's a testament to Grand Rapids' commitment to fostering a vibrant arts community and providing a platform for artists to showcase their work on an international stage. Whether you're an art enthusiast, a casual observer, or someone seeking inspiration, attending an ArtPrize event promises an enriching experience that transcends traditional boundaries and brings the transformative power of art to the heart of the city.

3.Take a stroll through the Frederik Meijer Gardens & Sculpture Park.

Taking a stroll through the Frederik Meijer Gardens & Sculpture Park in Grand Rapids is a serene and visually captivating experience. This expansive botanical garden and sculpture park seamlessly blends the beauty of nature with the allure of contemporary art. As you wander through meticulously landscaped gardens, you'll encounter a diverse array of plant species, seasonal blooms, and thematic landscapes that create a tranquil and immersive environment.

The sculpture park, a distinctive highlight of Frederik Meijer Gardens, features a remarkable collection of outdoor sculptures by renowned artists from around the world. Each sculpture is strategically placed to harmonize with the natural surroundings, offering a harmonious interplay between art and nature. The sculptures, ranging from classical to avant-garde, provide a visual feast that sparks contemplation and appreciation for the intersection of creativity and the environment.

Throughout your stroll, you may come across themed gardens such as the Japanese Garden, the English Perennial and Bulb Garden, or the Michigan Farm Garden, each offering a unique atmosphere and horticultural showcase. The Lena Meijer Tropical Conservatory provides a lush and tropical oasis, complete with exotic plants, water features, and vibrant displays.

Frederik Meijer Gardens & Sculpture Park also hosts seasonal exhibitions, events, and educational programs, making each visit a dynamic and evolving experience. The Richard and Helen DeVos Japanese Garden, a serene and contemplative space, is particularly noteworthy for its traditional design elements and peaceful ambiance.

Whether you're seeking a moment of tranquility, inspiration from world-class sculptures, or simply a delightful outdoor excursion, a stroll through Frederik Meijer Gardens & Sculpture Park offers a harmonious blend of nature, art, and cultural enrichment. It's a testament to Grand Rapids' commitment to providing a sanctuary where visitors can connect with the beauty of the natural world and the creative expressions of talented artists.

4. Visit the Grand Rapids Art Museum.

Visiting the Grand Rapids Art Museum (GRAM) is a cultural delight that offers a profound appreciation for the visual arts in the heart of downtown Grand Rapids. The museum, a striking architectural gem, houses an impressive collection of artworks spanning various periods, styles, and media. Upon entering, you're greeted by a welcoming and modern space that serves as a dynamic hub for artistic expression and community engagement.

The museum's permanent collection showcases an array of paintings, sculptures, and decorative arts, providing a comprehensive overview of both historic and contemporary artistic movements. From masterpieces by renowned painters to thought-provoking installations, GRAM offers a diverse range of visual experiences that cater to all tastes and interests. The curatorial choices reflect a commitment to fostering an inclusive and enriching environment for art enthusiasts and casual visitors alike.

GRAM is not only a haven for traditional visual arts but also a dynamic venue for special exhibitions, featuring works by local, national, and international artists. These exhibitions bring fresh perspectives and innovative approaches to the forefront, encouraging a continual dialogue about the evolving nature of art.

The museum's dedication to education and community outreach is evident in its diverse programming, including lectures, workshops, and family-friendly events. GRAM provides a space for cultural exchange and artistic exploration, contributing to the city's vibrant and evolving cultural landscape.

Whether you're an avid art collector, a casual observer, or someone seeking inspiration, a visit to the Grand Rapids Art Museum promises a thought-provoking and visually stimulating experience. It's a testament to the city's commitment to fostering a thriving arts community and providing a platform for the appreciation and celebration of creativity in all its forms.

5.Attend a live performance at the DeVos Performance Hall.

Attending a live performance at the DeVos Performance Hall in Grand Rapids is a captivating experience that combines the grandeur of the venue with the excitement of world-class performances. The hall, known for its elegant architecture and acoustically rich environment, sets the stage for a wide range of artistic expressions, from symphony concerts and Broadway shows to ballet performances and popular music acts.

The moment you step into the DeVos Performance Hall, you're greeted by a sense of sophistication and anticipation. The venue's design, with its ornate details and impeccable sightlines, creates an intimate yet majestic atmosphere that enhances the overall enjoyment of the performance. The state-of-the-art sound system ensures that every note, word, and nuance of the performance reaches the audience with clarity and precision.

Throughout the year, the hall hosts a diverse lineup of performances, attracting both local and internationally acclaimed artists. Whether you're attending a classical concert by the Grand Rapids Symphony, a Broadway production, a dance performance, or a contemporary music concert, the DeVos Performance Hall provides a stage for cultural enrichment and artistic excellence.

The hall's central location in downtown Grand Rapids adds to the overall experience, allowing attendees to explore the vibrant surroundings before or after the performance. Nearby restaurants, bars, and cultural attractions contribute to the city's lively arts scene, creating a well-rounded and memorable evening for patrons.

Attending a live performance at the DeVos Performance Hall is more than just a night out; it's an opportunity to immerse yourself in the arts, to be moved by the talents of performers, and to share in the collective appreciation of creativity. Whether you're a seasoned arts enthusiast or a first-time attendee, the DeVos Performance Hall offers a world-class venue for experiencing the magic of live entertainment in the heart of Grand Rapids.

6. Explore the historic Heritage Hill neighborhood.

Exploring the historic Heritage Hill neighborhood in Grand Rapids is a step back in time, offering a charming journey through well-preserved architecture, tree-lined streets, and a rich tapestry of the city's past. As one of the largest urban historic districts in the United States, Heritage Hill is renowned for its collection of beautifully restored 19th and early 20th-century homes, each with its own unique architectural character.

Wandering through the neighborhood, you'll discover a diverse array of architectural styles, including Italianate, Queen Anne, Colonial Revival, and more. Many of these stately homes boast intricate details, vibrant colors, and carefully manicured gardens, providing a visual feast for architecture enthusiasts and history buffs alike. The Heritage Hill Association, dedicated to preserving and promoting the neighborhood's heritage, has played a pivotal role in maintaining the authenticity and charm of this historic enclave.

In addition to the residential gems, Heritage Hill also features several historic landmarks, such as the Meyer May House, a Frank Lloyd Wright masterpiece, and the Voigt House Victorian Museum, offering a glimpse into the Victorian-era lifestyle. The neighborhood's streets are dotted with historic churches, schools, and other significant structures that contribute to the area's cultural and architectural significance.

Exploring Heritage Hill isn't just a visual delight; it's an opportunity to connect with the stories and the people who have shaped Grand Rapids over the centuries. The Heritage Hill neighborhood often hosts events like the Heritage Hill Home Tour, allowing visitors to step inside these historic homes and gain a deeper appreciation for the craftsmanship and history embedded in each dwelling.

Whether you're strolling down its leafy avenues during the vibrant fall foliage or admiring the historic homes adorned with twinkling lights during the holiday season, Heritage Hill exudes a timeless charm that encapsulates the essence of Grand Rapids' rich history. It's a living testament to the city's commitment to preserving its heritage and creating a space where the past seamlessly intertwines with the present.

7.Walk along the Grand River Heritage Trail.

Taking a leisurely walk along the Grand River Heritage Trail in Grand Rapids is a delightful outdoor experience that combines scenic beauty with a sense of tranquility. This picturesque trail, meandering along the banks of the Grand River, offers both residents and visitors an opportunity to connect with nature and appreciate the city's waterfront.

As you embark on your stroll, you'll be treated to panoramic views of the Grand River, with its gently flowing waters and lush riverbanks. The trail is designed to showcase the natural beauty of the area, providing a peaceful escape from the urban hustle. Tall trees, native vegetation, and the occasional wildlife create a serene environment, making it a perfect setting for a leisurely walk, jog, or bike ride.

One of the notable aspects of the Grand River Heritage Trail is its accessibility and inclusivity. Well-maintained pathways cater to individuals of all ages and abilities, ensuring that everyone can enjoy the beauty of the riverfront. Benches strategically placed along the trail invite you to pause, take in the surroundings, and perhaps enjoy a moment of reflection.

The trail also connects to various parks, green spaces, and other points of interest along the river, providing opportunities for picnics, birdwatching, or simply soaking up the peaceful ambiance. The evolving scenery, from open river views to shaded wooded areas, adds a dynamic element to the walking experience.

Whether you choose to explore the trail during the vibrant colors of autumn, the freshness of spring, or the warmth of summer, the Grand River Heritage Trail showcases Grand Rapids' commitment to preserving its natural resources and creating spaces for residents and visitors to engage with the outdoors. It's a place where the gentle rhythm of the river and the beauty of the surroundings invite you to unwind and appreciate the simple joys of a scenic walk along the water's edge.

8. Visit the Grand Rapids Public Museum.

Embarking on a visit to the Grand Rapids Public Museum is a journey into the past, an immersive exploration of history, science, and culture that unfolds within the captivating walls of this iconic institution. Situated along the banks of the Grand River, the museum offers a diverse range of exhibits and interactive displays that cater to a broad spectrum of interests and ages.

Upon entering, you'll find yourself surrounded by artifacts, dioramas, and exhibits that tell the story of Grand Rapids and its evolution through time. The museum's dedication to preserving and presenting local history is evident in its engaging displays, which span from the indigenous cultures that once inhabited the region to the industrial revolution that shaped the city's growth.

One of the highlights of the Grand Rapids Public Museum is the Streets of Old Grand Rapids exhibit, a meticulously recreated streetscape from the late 19th century that provides a vivid glimpse into daily life during that era. The carousel, a cherished feature, adds a touch of whimsy and nostalgia to the experience, making it a favorite for visitors of all ages.

The museum's commitment to science education is evident in its interactive exhibits, such as the Whales: Giants of the Deep exhibit and the West Michigan Habitats display. These areas offer hands-on experiences and educational opportunities that engage visitors in the wonders of the natural world.

A visit to the Grand Rapids Public Museum is not only an exploration of the city's history but also an invitation to delve into broader topics, from anthropology and paleontology to cultural diversity and innovation. The Chaffee Planetarium, housed within the museum, provides a celestial journey through space, adding an extra layer of fascination to the overall experience.

Whether you're a local resident looking to deepen your connection to Grand Rapids' heritage or a visitor eager to uncover the cultural tapestry of the region, the Grand Rapids Public Museum stands as a testament to the city's commitment to education, preservation, and the celebration of the diverse narratives that have shaped its identity over the years.

9.Attend a concert or event at Van Andel Arena.

Attending a concert or event at Van Andel Arena in Grand Rapids is an electrifying experience that combines the thrill of live entertainment with the state-of-the-art amenities of this renowned venue. Nestled in the heart of downtown Grand Rapids, Van Andel Arena stands as a vibrant hub for music, sports, and cultural events, drawing crowds from across the region.

The moment you step into the arena, you're enveloped in an atmosphere of anticipation and excitement. The venue's modern design and impressive capacity create an immersive setting for a diverse array of events, from blockbuster concerts and high-energy sporting events to family shows and theatrical performances.

Van Andel Arena has played host to some of the biggest names in the music industry, bringing a dynamic range of genres to its stage. Whether you're a fan of rock, pop, country, or hip-hop, the arena's concert lineup caters to a broad spectrum of musical tastes. The acoustics and lighting design enhance the overall concert experience, ensuring that every note and visual element resonates with the audience.

In addition to musical performances, the arena regularly hosts sporting events that capture the competitive spirit of Grand Rapids. Whether it's a hockey game, basketball match, or other sporting spectacles, Van Andel Arena provides a top-notch venue for both athletes and spectators.

The versatility of the arena extends to family-friendly shows, comedy performances, and community events, making it a central gathering place for diverse entertainment experiences. Its central location in the downtown area adds to the allure, allowing attendees to explore the vibrant surroundings before or after the event.

Attending a concert or event at Van Andel Arena is more than just a night out; it's a communal celebration of culture and entertainment. The venue's commitment to hosting world-class events reflects Grand Rapids' status as a dynamic and culturally rich city, inviting residents and visitors alike to partake in the shared excitement of live performances in the heart of West Michigan.

10.Experience the John Ball Zoo.

Experiencing the John Ball Zoo in Grand Rapids is a delightful adventure that brings together the wonders of the animal kingdom with immersive exhibits and family-friendly attractions. Nestled on the west side of the city, the zoo provides a captivating and educational environment where visitors of all ages can connect with wildlife from around the globe.

Upon entering the John Ball Zoo, you'll find yourself surrounded by lush landscapes and thoughtfully designed habitats that prioritize the well-being and conservation of the animals. The zoo is home to a diverse array of species, ranging from iconic African elephants and playful primates to colorful birds and exotic reptiles. The zoo's commitment to conservation is evident in its efforts to create environments that mimic the natural habitats of its residents.

One of the highlights of the John Ball Zoo is the Crawford Tigers of the Realm exhibit, where majestic Amur tigers roam in a sprawling space that allows for up-close observations. The Idema Forest Realm provides an immersive experience, allowing visitors to walk through a forested area and encounter animals like red pandas, otters, and wallabies in a more naturalistic setting.

The zoo also offers engaging and interactive experiences, such as the Treasures of the Tropics exhibit featuring tropical birds and reptiles, and the Budgie Aviary, where visitors can feed and interact with colorful parakeets. The playful atmosphere of the Treetop Outpost and the family-friendly touchpools at the Living Shores Aquarium add to the overall charm of the zoo.

Education is a key focus at the John Ball Zoo, with various programs and events designed to enhance visitors' understanding of wildlife conservation and ecological sustainability. The Bissell Treehouse, an architectural gem within the zoo, provides a unique learning space with panoramic views of the surrounding area.

Whether you're exploring the zoo with family, enjoying a solo visit, or participating in one of the zoo's special events, the John Ball Zoo promises a memorable and enriching experience. It's a testament to Grand Rapids' dedication to fostering a connection between people and wildlife, promoting conservation awareness, and creating a space where the magic of the animal kingdom comes to life.

11.Take a scenic drive along the M-22 route.

Embarking on a scenic drive along the M-22 route in Michigan is a breathtaking journey that winds its way through some of the state's most picturesque landscapes, offering travelers a visual feast of natural beauty and coastal charm. Starting near Manistee, the M-22 route traces the western shore of Michigan, guiding drivers along Lake Michigan and showcasing the region's diverse scenery.

As you set out on this road trip, you'll be treated to panoramic views of the Great Lakes, with the shimmering waters of Lake Michigan accompanying your drive. The route meanders through charming small towns, such as Arcadia and Frankfort, each with its own unique character and attractions.

The M-22 journey takes you through the iconic Sleeping Bear Dunes National Lakeshore, where towering sand dunes offer mesmerizing vistas of Lake Michigan. The Pierce Stocking Scenic Drive within the park provides elevated viewpoints that are perfect for taking in the breathtaking scenery.

Continuing north, the route leads through the quaint village of Glen Arbor, known for its artsy shops and proximity to the crystal-clear waters of Glen Lake. The drive then takes you to Leland, a historic fishing town with a picturesque harbor and the iconic Fishtown district, where weathered shanties evoke the area's maritime history.

As you drive through the Leelanau Peninsula, vineyards and orchards come into view, contributing to the region's reputation as a burgeoning wine and agriculture destination. Numerous wineries dot the landscape, offering opportunities for tastings and scenic stops.

The M-22 route reaches its northern terminus in Northport, a charming town with a welcoming harbor. The journey offers a mix of forested stretches, coastal panoramas, and charming communities, making it an ideal route for those seeking a serene and visually captivating road trip.

Whether you're driving during the vibrant colors of autumn, the blossoming beauty of spring, or the warmth of summer, the M-22 scenic drive encapsulates the natural splendor that Michigan has to offer. It's a route that beckons explorers to slow down, savor the journey, and appreciate the ever-changing landscapes that unfold along the way.

12.Attend a game or event at Fifth Third Ballpark.

Attending a game or event at Fifth Third Ballpark in Grand Rapids is a quintessential experience for sports enthusiasts and families alike. Home to the West Michigan Whitecaps, a Minor League Baseball team, the ballpark combines the thrill of America's favorite pastime with a welcoming and family-friendly atmosphere.

As you approach Fifth Third Ballpark, you'll be greeted by the excitement of the game day ambiance – the crack of the bat, the cheers of the crowd, and the aroma of ballpark concessions. The venue offers a classic baseball experience with modern amenities, ensuring that spectators can enjoy the game in comfort.

The West Michigan Whitecaps, affiliated with the Detroit Tigers, provide an opportunity to watch talented players as they showcase their skills and passion for the sport. The intimate setting of the ballpark allows fans to get up close to the action, making it an ideal environment for both die-hard baseball enthusiasts and those attending their first game.

In addition to baseball games, Fifth Third Ballpark hosts a variety of events throughout the year, including concerts, festivals, and community gatherings. The versatility of the venue transforms it into a lively hub for entertainment beyond the baseball season, contributing to its status as a community focal point.

Family-friendly features such as the Pepsi Stadium Club, a playground area for kids, and themed nights add to the overall appeal of Fifth Third Ballpark. The venue's commitment to creating a positive and inclusive experience for fans of all ages makes it an ideal destination for group outings, celebrations, or simply a fun day at the ballpark.

Whether you're cheering for the home team, enjoying a summer evening with friends and family, or attending a special event, Fifth Third Ballpark embodies the spirit of community and the timeless joy of baseball. It's a place where the crack of the bat and the camaraderie of the crowd create lasting memories for those who embrace the tradition and excitement of America's favorite pastime.

13.Explore local breweries on the Beer City Ale Trail.

Embarking on a journey along the Beer City Ale Trail in Grand Rapids is a craft beer enthusiast's dream, offering a delightful exploration of the city's vibrant and renowned craft beer scene. As you traverse the Ale Trail, you'll discover a diverse array of breweries, each contributing its unique flavors, styles, and atmospheres to the rich tapestry of Grand Rapids' brewing culture.

The Beer City Ale Trail showcases the city's designation as "Beer City, USA," a title it earned thanks to its impressive concentration of craft breweries. The trail guides you through neighborhoods, downtown districts, and even the outskirts of the city, providing a comprehensive and immersive experience for beer connoisseurs and casual enthusiasts alike.

Starting your journey, you might explore the breweries clustered in the vibrant downtown area, each with its distinctive character. From established names like Founders Brewing Co., known for its bold and innovative brews, to smaller gems like Grand Rapids Brewing Company, the trail offers a diverse range of craft beer options.

Venturing beyond downtown, you may find yourself in the East Hills neighborhood, home to breweries like Brewery Vivant, housed in a renovated funeral chapel, providing a unique ambiance and a focus on Belgian-inspired beers. The Eastown neighborhood also offers hidden gems, such as Harmony Brewing Company, known for its cozy atmosphere and creative pizza pairings.

The West Side of Grand Rapids boasts its own collection of breweries, with destinations like New Holland Brewing – The Knickerbocker, offering an expansive space with a rooftop bar and a commitment to locally sourced ingredients.

Beyond the urban core, the Beer City Ale Trail leads to suburban and rural breweries, each contributing to the region's diverse beer offerings. From the rural charm of Rockford Brewing Company to the innovative beers of Perrin Brewing Company in Comstock Park, the trail showcases the creativity and craftsmanship that define West Michigan's brewing culture.

Whether you're a fan of hop-forward IPAs, rich stouts, or experimental brews, the Beer City Ale Trail provides a tasting journey that caters to all palates. The trail's comprehensive map and guides make it easy to plan your route, ensuring you can savor the flavors, learn about the brewing process, and appreciate the warm hospitality that defines Grand Rapids' reputation as a beer destination. So, lace up your walking shoes, hop on a bike, or embark on a designated driver-led adventure to explore the Beer City Ale Trail and discover why Grand Rapids has earned its well-deserved reputation as a haven for craft beer enthusiasts.

14. Visit the Grand Rapids Children's Museum.

Visiting the Grand Rapids Children's Museum is an immersive and educational experience designed specifically for young minds, offering a dynamic space where children can engage in hands-on learning through play and exploration. Located in the heart of downtown Grand Rapids, the museum provides a safe and stimulating environment that encourages creativity, curiosity, and social interaction.

Upon entering the Grand Rapids Children's Museum, you'll discover a vibrant and interactive space filled with exhibits and activities tailored to different age groups. The museum's philosophy revolves around the idea that children learn best through play, and each exhibit is crafted to foster their cognitive, emotional, and physical development.

The various exhibits at the Children's Museum cover a wide range of themes, from science and technology to arts and culture. Children can explore a pretend market, engage in water play, experiment with building blocks, and immerse themselves in imaginative play scenarios. The museum's emphasis on hands-on experiences allows children to learn about the world around them in a fun and interactive manner.

Special programs and events are often held at the museum, including workshops, storytimes, and themed activities that align with educational goals. The museum's commitment to early childhood education is evident in its dedication to providing a dynamic and enriching space where families can bond and children can develop essential skills.

One of the notable features of the Grand Rapids Children's Museum is its emphasis on inclusivity, ensuring that all children, regardless of ability or background, can participate and enjoy the exhibits. The museum's staff is trained to create a welcoming environment for families and to facilitate positive learning experiences.

Whether you're a local resident looking for a fun and educational outing for your children or a visitor seeking a family-friendly destination in Grand Rapids, the Children's Museum provides an invaluable resource for fostering a love of learning and exploration in young ones. It's a place where laughter, curiosity, and discovery intersect, creating lasting memories for families and contributing to the educational foundation of the next generation.

15.Go hiking at Millennium Park.

Embarking on a hiking adventure at Millennium Park in Grand Rapids promises a refreshing outdoor experience, combining natural beauty with recreational activities in a sprawling urban park setting. Millennium Park, one of the largest urban parks in West Michigan, spans over 1,500 acres and offers a diverse range of trails, water features, and picturesque landscapes.

As you set out on your hike, you'll find well-maintained trails that wind through woodlands, wetlands, and open spaces. The park's trail system caters to various skill levels, providing options for both casual strollers and avid hikers. Whether you're seeking a leisurely nature walk or a more challenging hike, Millennium Park offers a network of interconnected trails that allow you to tailor your outdoor experience to your preferences.

One of the highlights of hiking at Millennium Park is the chance to explore the park's three man-made lakes, providing serene views and opportunities for birdwatching. The park's water features add a tranquil element to the hiking experience, and you might encounter local wildlife while traversing the scenic paths.

The Fred Meijer Millennium Trail, a 22-mile loop that encircles the park, offers a longer and more immersive hiking option for those looking to cover more ground. Along this trail, you'll encounter diverse ecosystems, including forests, prairies, and wetlands, showcasing the park's commitment to environmental preservation.

The park also features amenities such as boardwalks, bridges, and overlooks, allowing hikers to appreciate the natural beauty and diverse landscapes. Additionally, Millennium Park provides recreational activities beyond hiking, including biking, fishing, and boating, making it a versatile destination for outdoor enthusiasts.

Whether you choose to hike through shaded woodlands, enjoy the scenic beauty of lakeside trails, or simply relish the tranquility of nature, Millennium Park offers a rejuvenating escape within the city limits. It's a place where the beauty of the outdoors converges with recreational opportunities, providing a welcoming and accessible space for individuals, families, and nature enthusiasts to connect with the natural wonders of Grand Rapids.

16.Attend the Tulip Time Festival in Holland (near Grand Rapids).

Attending the Tulip Time Festival in Holland, located near Grand Rapids, is a vibrant and enchanting experience that celebrates the beauty of spring, Dutch heritage, and the breathtaking display of tulips. Held annually in May, this festival transforms the charming city of Holland into a kaleidoscope of colors, cultural performances, and community spirit.

The Tulip Time Festival is renowned for its stunning tulip displays, with millions of tulips blooming across the city's parks, gardens, and streets. The iconic Windmill Island Gardens, home to the historic De Zwaan windmill, is a centerpiece of the festival, adorned with tulip beds in a stunning array of hues. Visitors can stroll through the meticulously landscaped gardens, capturing the beauty of the tulips against the backdrop of the working windmill and scenic water features.

One of the festival's highlights is the Volksparade, a grand procession featuring authentic Dutch costumes, traditional Dutch dance performances, and impressive floats adorned with tulips. The colorful parade winds through the streets of downtown Holland, creating a festive atmosphere that showcases the city's Dutch heritage and community pride.

Tulip Time also offers a variety of events and activities, including artisan markets, Dutch food tastings, and live entertainment. The streets come alive with street performers, music, and cultural demonstrations, creating a lively and festive ambiance throughout the festival.

In addition to enjoying the tulip displays and cultural events, attendees can explore the charming downtown area, lined with boutique shops, galleries, and restaurants. The festival provides a perfect opportunity to savor Dutch treats, indulge in local cuisine, and shop for unique souvenirs.

Whether you're a flower enthusiast, a fan of cultural celebrations, or someone simply seeking a delightful springtime experience, the Tulip Time Festival in Holland is a must-visit. It's a celebration of nature's beauty, community spirit, and the rich Dutch heritage that has left an indelible mark on this picturesque city near Grand Rapids.

17.Explore the Medical Mile district.

Exploring the Medical Mile district in Grand Rapids unveils a dynamic and evolving hub of healthcare, research, and innovation. Located in the heart of the city, this corridor is home to world-class medical institutions, cutting-edge research facilities, and a thriving healthcare ecosystem that collectively contributes to the region's reputation as a center of medical excellence.

One of the prominent features of the Medical Mile is the presence of the Michigan State University College of Human Medicine, which collaborates with various healthcare partners to advance medical education, research, and patient care. The medical school's facilities on the Medical Mile foster a collaborative environment where students, faculty, and healthcare professionals work together to address health challenges and contribute to medical advancements.

Van Andel Institute, a renowned biomedical research and science education facility, is another key institution along the Medical Mile. The institute is dedicated to advancing medical research, particularly in the fields of cancer, neurodegenerative diseases, and epigenetics. Its state-of-the-art research facilities attract scientists and researchers from around the world.

The Medical Mile is also home to several major hospitals, including Spectrum Health, one of the largest healthcare systems in West Michigan. Spectrum Health facilities on the Medical Mile encompass specialized care centers, research institutes, and educational spaces, creating a comprehensive healthcare environment.

As you explore the district, you'll encounter modern architecture, research facilities, and educational institutions seamlessly integrated with green spaces and pedestrian-friendly areas. The design of the Medical Mile fosters collaboration and innovation, emphasizing the integration of research, education, and clinical care.

Beyond healthcare and research, the district is surrounded by amenities that cater to the needs of students, healthcare professionals, and the community. Restaurants, cafes, and green spaces offer opportunities for relaxation and socialization, creating a well-rounded and dynamic environment.

The Medical Mile district is not only a testament to Grand Rapids' commitment to healthcare excellence but also a symbol of the city's continuous efforts to position itself at the forefront of medical innovation and education. It serves as a hub where medical professionals, researchers, and educators converge, driving advancements in healthcare and contributing to the well-being of the community.

18.Attend a Broadway Grand Rapids performance.

Attending a Broadway Grand Rapids performance is an exciting and culturally enriching experience that brings the magic of Broadway to the vibrant arts scene of Grand Rapids. Broadway Grand Rapids, a nonprofit organization, brings a diverse selection of Broadway touring productions to the city, offering residents and visitors the opportunity to enjoy world-class theatrical performances.

The venue for Broadway Grand Rapids performances may vary, but it often takes place at the DeVos Performance Hall, a stunning venue in downtown Grand Rapids known for its elegant architecture and exceptional acoustics. The hall provides an intimate and immersive setting, allowing audiences to fully experience the spectacle and drama of Broadway productions.

The Broadway Grand Rapids lineup features a range of acclaimed shows, including beloved classics, contemporary hits, and Tony Award-winning productions. Whether it's a timeless musical, a thought-provoking drama, or a lively and entertaining performance, each Broadway Grand Rapids production is carefully curated to appeal to a broad audience with diverse tastes.

Attending a Broadway Grand Rapids performance means experiencing the professionalism, talent, and spectacle associated with Broadway productions. From the elaborate sets and costumes to the exceptional performances by seasoned actors, each show is a testament to the organization's dedication to bringing the best of Broadway to West Michigan.

The excitement of a Broadway Grand Rapids performance extends beyond the stage, as attendees often have the opportunity to engage with the local arts community, explore downtown Grand Rapids, and enjoy the cultural amenities that surround the DeVos Performance Hall.

Whether you're a seasoned theatergoer or someone attending their first Broadway show, the experience of witnessing a live performance in the heart of Grand Rapids is sure to leave a lasting impression. Broadway Grand Rapids contributes to the city's vibrant arts and entertainment landscape, ensuring that residents and visitors alike have access to the magic and wonder of Broadway right in their own community.

19.Enjoy a picnic at Riverside Park.

Picnicking at Riverside Park in Grand Rapids is a delightful way to experience nature, enjoy outdoor activities, and savor the scenic beauty of this expansive urban park. Located along the Grand River, Riverside Park offers a serene and picturesque setting that invites visitors to unwind, connect with the outdoors, and create lasting memories.

As you plan your picnic at Riverside Park, consider the following aspects to enhance your experience:

Scenic Riverside Setting: Choose a spot along the riverbanks or in one of the park's grassy areas to enjoy the calming views of the Grand River. The tranquil ambiance creates a perfect backdrop for a relaxing picnic.

Picnic Facilities: Riverside Park is equipped with picnic tables, shelters, and open spaces, providing convenient areas for picnicking. Some areas may require reservations for larger groups, so it's a good idea to check in advance.

Riverwalk and Trails: Explore the park's Riverwalk and trails before or after your picnic. Riverside Park offers walking and biking trails that wind through wooded areas and along the river, providing an opportunity to connect with nature and enjoy a leisurely stroll.

Play Areas: If you're picnicking with family, Riverside Park features play areas for children, including playgrounds and open spaces for games and activities. It's a great way to keep everyone entertained.

Wildlife Watching: Keep an eye out for local wildlife, including birds and waterfowl. The park's natural surroundings create a habitat for various species, adding to the overall outdoor experience.

Seasonal Considerations: Depending on the season, Riverside Park offers different scenic views. In the spring, blooming flowers and budding trees add color to the landscape, while fall brings vibrant foliage. Each season provides a unique and captivating backdrop for your picnic.

Pack a Picnic Basket: Bring your favorite snacks, sandwiches, and refreshments to enjoy during your picnic. Don't forget essentials like a blanket, utensils, and napkins.

Relax and Unwind: Take the opportunity to relax, unwind, and appreciate the natural beauty around you. Whether you're with friends, family, or enjoying some quiet time alone, Riverside Park provides a peaceful escape within the city.

Remember to adhere to any park rules or regulations and be mindful of leaving no trace by properly disposing of your picnic waste. With its scenic charm and recreational amenities, Riverside Park offers an idyllic setting for a memorable and enjoyable picnic experience in Grand Rapids.

20.Explore the Fulton Street Farmers Market.

Exploring the Fulton Street Farmers Market in Grand Rapids is a vibrant and sensory-rich experience that immerses visitors in the local agricultural bounty and community spirit. Nestled in the historic district, the market has been a staple in the community since 1922, showcasing the region's agricultural richness and providing a lively space for residents to connect with local farmers and artisans.

Here's what you can expect when exploring the Fulton Street Farmers Market:

Fresh Produce and Local Goods: The market is a treasure trove of fresh, locally grown produce, including fruits, vegetables, herbs, and flowers. Local farmers and vendors proudly display their seasonal offerings, allowing visitors to indulge in the flavors of West Michigan.

Artisanal Products: Beyond fresh produce, the market features a diverse array of artisanal products. From handmade crafts and artisan cheeses to baked goods and locally sourced honey, there's a wide variety of goods crafted by local artisans and producers.

Community Atmosphere: The Fulton Street Farmers Market is not just a place to shop; it's a community gathering spot. The lively atmosphere, filled with the sounds of conversations, laughter, and live music, creates a sense of camaraderie among vendors and visitors alike.

Food Trucks and Prepared Foods: In addition to raw ingredients, the market often hosts food trucks and stalls offering delicious ready-to-eat items. It's an opportunity to savor local flavors and try something new while exploring the market.

Seasonal Offerings: The market's offerings change with the seasons, reflecting the agricultural calendar. Whether it's the vibrant colors of summer berries, the abundance of fall harvest, or the freshness of spring greens, each visit to the market brings a new palette of flavors and aromas.

Educational Opportunities: The market occasionally hosts educational events, workshops, and demonstrations. This provides an opportunity for visitors to learn about sustainable farming practices, cooking techniques, and the importance of supporting local agriculture.

Historical Charm: The Fulton Street Farmers Market is located in a historic district, and the market itself has retained its original charm. The market's rustic pavilion and open-air stalls contribute to the nostalgic and authentic feel of the space.

Community Engagement: The market is a hub for community engagement, fostering connections between farmers, artisans, and residents. It serves as a platform for supporting local businesses and building a sustainable and resilient local food system.

Exploring the Fulton Street Farmers Market is not just a shopping excursion; it's a multisensory journey through the flavors, aromas, and community spirit of West Michigan. Whether you're a local resident or a visitor, the market offers a genuine and enjoyable experience that celebrates the region's agricultural heritage and the vitality of the community.

21.Visit the UICA (Urban Institute for Contemporary Arts).

Visiting the Urban Institute for Contemporary Arts (UICA) in Grand Rapids promises an immersive and thought-provoking experience in the realm of contemporary art. Situated in the heart of downtown Grand Rapids, the UICA is a dynamic cultural hub dedicated to showcasing innovative and cutting-edge works across various artistic disciplines.

Here's what you can expect when visiting the UICA:

Exhibitions: The UICA regularly hosts a diverse range of contemporary art exhibitions, featuring works by local, national, and international artists. The exhibitions span various mediums, including painting, sculpture, photography, new media, and installations, providing a comprehensive view of contemporary artistic practices.

Film Screenings: In addition to visual arts, the UICA has a strong focus on film as an art form. The UICA regularly screens independent and international films, documentaries, and avant-garde cinema, contributing to the city's cinematic landscape.

Cinema Studies: The UICA often engages in educational initiatives related to cinema studies, offering programs, discussions, and workshops that delve into the world of filmmaking and storytelling through moving images.

Educational Programs: The UICA is committed to fostering art appreciation and understanding. As part of this commitment, the institute conducts educational programs, workshops, and artist talks that allow visitors to engage directly with the creative process and gain insights into contemporary art practices.

ArtPrize Venue: During the annual ArtPrize event in Grand Rapids, the UICA serves as a venue for showcasing a curated selection of artworks. This provides a unique opportunity for artists to display their creations in a contemporary art setting.

Café and Retail Space: The UICA building often features a café and retail space, creating a welcoming environment for visitors to relax, enjoy refreshments, and browse unique art-related merchandise.

Architecture and Design: The UICA's building itself is an architectural gem, contributing to the vibrant urban landscape of Grand Rapids. The design of the space is intentional, creating an environment that complements and enhances the contemporary art experience.

Community Engagement: The UICA actively engages with the local community, collaborating with artists, schools, and organizations to promote accessibility to contemporary art. This community-oriented approach aligns with Grand Rapids' commitment to fostering a thriving and inclusive arts scene.

Whether you're a seasoned art enthusiast or someone curious to explore the cutting edge of contemporary creativity, a visit to the UICA offers a stimulating and enriching experience. It's a space where art comes to life, challenges conventions, and invites visitors to explore the ever-evolving landscape of contemporary artistic expression in the heart of Grand Rapids.

22.Go kayaking on the Grand River.

Embarking on a kayaking adventure on the Grand River in Grand Rapids promises a scenic and refreshing outdoor experience, allowing you to explore the city from a unique and tranquil perspective. The Grand River, winding through the heart of the city, offers paddlers a blend of urban and natural landscapes, creating an immersive and enjoyable kayaking journey.

Here's what you can expect when kayaking on the Grand River:

Rental Facilities: Several outfitters in the Grand Rapids area provide kayak rentals, making it convenient for both experienced paddlers and beginners to enjoy a day on the water. These facilities typically offer single and tandem kayaks, life vests, and basic instructions for a safe and enjoyable experience.

Launch Points: Choose from various launch points along the Grand River, depending on the length and type of kayaking experience you desire. Popular launch points include Riverside Park, Grand River Park, and Millennium Park. Each offers a unique starting point with access to different sections of the river.

Urban and Natural Scenery: Kayaking on the Grand River provides a mix of urban and natural scenery. Paddle through downtown areas with skyline views, pass beneath historic bridges, and then transition into more secluded stretches surrounded by trees and wildlife.

Downtown Views: As you navigate through the heart of Grand Rapids, you'll have the opportunity to enjoy views of iconic landmarks, public art installations, and the city's vibrant atmosphere. It's a distinctive way to appreciate the urban landscape from the water.

Wildlife Watching: The Grand River is home to various bird species and other wildlife. Keep an eye out for herons, ducks, turtles, and perhaps even fish swimming beneath your kayak. The natural habitats along the riverbanks create opportunities for wildlife encounters.

Peaceful Retreat: Despite being in the midst of a bustling city, kayaking on the Grand River can offer a peaceful retreat. The gentle flow of the river, combined with the natural surroundings, creates a serene and meditative experience on the water.

Flexible Routes: Depending on your skill level and the time you have, you can choose from different kayaking routes. Opt for a short and leisurely paddle or embark on a longer adventure, exploring various stretches of the Grand River.

Group or Solo Excursions: Kayaking on the Grand River is suitable for both solo paddlers and groups. Whether you prefer a quiet solo journey or a social outing with friends or family, the river accommodates a variety of preferences.

Before setting out, it's advisable to check weather conditions, river levels, and any safety guidelines provided by the rental facility. Whether you're a seasoned kayaker or trying it for the first time, kayaking on the Grand River provides a refreshing and enjoyable way to connect with nature and the vibrant city of Grand Rapids.

23.Attend a performance at the Actors' Theatre Grand Rapids.

Attending a performance at Actors' Theatre Grand Rapids promises a captivating and immersive theatrical experience, showcasing the city's vibrant arts and culture scene. Located in the heart of Grand Rapids, Actors' Theatre is a community-driven theater company that has been enriching the local stage for decades, providing audiences with thought-provoking and entertaining productions.

Here's what you can expect when attending a performance at Actors' Theatre:

Diverse Productions: Actors' Theatre is known for its commitment to presenting a diverse range of productions, including contemporary plays, classic dramas, and innovative works. The theater's repertoire reflects a dedication to artistic excellence and a desire to engage audiences with a variety of theatrical genres.

Talented Performers: The productions at Actors' Theatre feature talented and dedicated performers, often drawn from the local community. The actors bring characters to life with authenticity and passion, contributing to the immersive and high-quality nature of the performances.

Intimate Setting: The theater's intimate setting provides an up-close and personal experience for the audience. Whether you're attending a dramatic play, a comedy, or a musical, the proximity to the stage enhances the emotional impact and connection with the performers.

Community Engagement: Actors' Theatre actively engages with the local community, fostering a sense of inclusivity and collaboration. The theater often partners with local artists, directors, and organizations, contributing to the cultural richness of Grand Rapids.

Innovative Productions: Beyond traditional performances, Actors' Theatre occasionally stages innovative and experimental productions, pushing the boundaries of traditional theater. These performances provide a unique and thought-provoking experience for theater enthusiasts.

Educational Initiatives: The theater is involved in educational initiatives, offering programs, workshops, and opportunities for aspiring actors and theater enthusiasts to deepen their understanding of the performing arts. This commitment to education contributes to the development of the local arts community.

Accessible Venue: The venue itself is designed to be accessible and welcoming to all audience members. Whether you're a seasoned theatergoer or attending your first performance, Actors' Theatre provides an inviting atmosphere for diverse audiences.

Seasonal Programming: Actors' Theatre typically offers seasonal programming, featuring a lineup of productions throughout the year. This variety allows audiences to explore different genres and themes, ensuring there's something for everyone.

Attending a performance at Actors' Theatre Grand Rapids is not just a night at the theater; it's an opportunity to engage with the local arts community, experience compelling storytelling, and support the creative endeavors of the talented individuals who contribute to the vibrant cultural tapestry of Grand Rapids.

24. Take a brewery tour at Founders Brewing Co.

Embarking on a brewery tour at Founders Brewing Co. in Grand Rapids is a flavorful journey into the heart of one of Michigan's most renowned craft breweries. Founders Brewing Co. is celebrated for its innovative brews, commitment to quality, and the inviting atmosphere of its taproom. A brewery tour provides an insider's look into the beer-making process and the rich history of Founders.

Here's what you can expect on a brewery tour at Founders Brewing Co.:

Guided Exploration: Led by knowledgeable guides, the brewery tour takes you through the various stages of the brewing process. From the sourcing of ingredients to the intricacies of fermentation and bottling, you'll gain insights into the craftsmanship behind Founders' exceptional beers.

Historical Narratives: Founders Brewing Co. has a rich history dating back to its founding in 1997. During the tour, you'll likely hear fascinating stories about the brewery's origins, growth, and the evolution of its beer offerings. Understanding the brewery's journey adds depth to the tasting experience.

Production Facility Visit: The tour often includes a visit to the production facility, where you can witness the scale and efficiency of Founders' brewing operations. It's an opportunity to see the machinery, tanks, and barrels that contribute to the creation of their diverse beer lineup.

Tasting Sessions: A highlight of any brewery tour is the tasting session. Sample a variety of Founders' signature and seasonal beers, gaining an appreciation for the different styles and flavors that make their brews distinctive. Guides may provide insights into the unique characteristics of each beer.

Taproom Atmosphere: Following the tour, many brewery tours conclude in the taproom. Founders Brewing Co. offers a welcoming and convivial atmosphere where you can relax, enjoy additional tastings, and perhaps pair your beers with some delicious food from their menu.

Exclusive Offerings: Depending on the tour package or the time of your visit, you may have the chance to try limited or exclusive releases. Founders is known for its experimentation and creativity in brewing, so there's often something new and exciting to discover.

Merchandise and Souvenirs: The brewery tour typically concludes with a visit to the merchandise area. Here, you can browse a selection of Founders Brewing Co. branded merchandise, including glassware, apparel, and other souvenirs, allowing you to take a piece of the brewery home with you.

Community and Events: Founders Brewing Co. often hosts events and gatherings, fostering a sense of community among beer enthusiasts. Check the brewery's schedule to see if there are any special events or festivals aligning with your visit.

Whether you're a seasoned beer connoisseur or someone eager to learn more about the art of brewing, a brewery tour at Founders Brewing Co. provides a well-rounded and enjoyable experience. It's a chance to taste exceptional beers, uncover the brewery's stories, and immerse yourself in the craft beer culture that defines Grand Rapids.

25.Go ice skating at Rosa Parks Circle in winter.

Ice skating at Rosa Parks Circle in winter is a festive and exhilarating experience that captures the essence of winter in downtown Grand Rapids. Rosa Parks Circle, located in the heart of the city, transforms into a charming outdoor ice skating rink during the winter months, providing a picturesque setting for both locals and visitors to enjoy this classic winter activity.

Here's what you can expect when ice skating at Rosa Parks Circle:

Outdoor Skating Rink: The rink at Rosa Parks Circle is an open-air skating rink, allowing skaters to enjoy the crisp winter air and the surrounding urban landscape. The rink is typically surrounded by seasonal decorations and festive lighting, creating a cheerful ambiance.

Iconic Location: Rosa Parks Circle serves as a central gathering place in downtown Grand Rapids. Surrounded by shops, restaurants, and cultural institutions, the location adds to the vibrancy of the skating experience. The area is known for its welcoming atmosphere and community events.

Skating Rentals: Whether you're a seasoned skater or a first-timer, Rosa Parks Circle offers skate rentals on-site. This makes it accessible for everyone, and you can easily get outfitted with the necessary gear to enjoy your time on the ice.

Seasonal Decorations: During the winter season, Rosa Parks Circle is often adorned with seasonal decorations, adding a touch of holiday charm. The festive surroundings enhance the overall winter wonderland atmosphere.

Music and Events: Skating at Rosa Parks Circle is often accompanied by music playing in the background. The rink occasionally hosts special events, themed skate nights, or live performances, adding an extra layer of entertainment to the skating experience.

Family-Friendly Atmosphere: The outdoor rink at Rosa Parks Circle is a popular destination for families. Whether you're skating with loved ones or enjoying the sight of families gliding across the ice, the atmosphere is family-friendly and welcoming.

City Views: As you skate, you'll have the opportunity to enjoy views of the surrounding cityscape. The urban setting, combined with the seasonal decorations, creates a unique and memorable backdrop for your skating adventure.

Hot Beverages and Snacks: Nearby vendors or concessions often offer hot beverages and snacks, providing an opportunity to warm up and refuel during or after your time on the ice.

Whether you're a skilled figure skater or someone lacing up skates for the first time, ice skating at Rosa Parks Circle offers a joyful and festive winter experience. It's a tradition that brings the community together and allows individuals of all ages to embrace the magic of winter in downtown Grand Rapids.

26.Attend a concert at the Intersection.

Attending a concert at the Intersection in Grand Rapids is a high-energy and immersive experience that showcases the city's vibrant music scene. The Intersection, located in the Heartside neighborhood, is a renowned live music venue known for hosting a diverse range of musical acts, from emerging artists to established bands. Here's what you can expect when attending a concert at the Intersection:

Varied Music Genres: The Intersection is known for its eclectic lineup, featuring performances across various music genres. Whether you're into rock, hip-hop, electronic, indie, or alternative music, the venue caters to a wide range of musical tastes, making it a dynamic hub for music enthusiasts.

Intimate Setting: The venue's design provides an intimate and up-close experience for concertgoers. With a capacity that allows for a close connection between the audience and the performers, attending a concert at the Intersection offers a more personal and immersive atmosphere compared to larger venues.

Live Bands and Artists: The Intersection has hosted both emerging and well-established artists. Local bands, regional acts, and national touring artists frequently grace the stage, contributing to the venue's reputation as a key player in the live music scene.

Standing Room and General Admission: The concert experience at the Intersection often involves standing room and general admission, allowing for a more fluid and energetic atmosphere. This setup encourages concertgoers to move, dance, and fully engage with the live music performance.

Full-Service Bar: The venue typically features a full-service bar where patrons can enjoy a variety of beverages while watching the show. This adds to the overall social and entertainment aspect of the concert experience.

Community Vibe: The Intersection has become a community hub for music lovers in Grand Rapids. Its role in supporting local and national acts fosters a sense of community among attendees, creating a shared space for the celebration of live music.

Historic Venue: The Intersection has a rich history, with the building dating back to the early 20th century. Its evolution into a premier live music venue adds a layer of historical charm to the concert experience.

Special Events and Theme Nights: In addition to regular concerts, the Intersection occasionally hosts special events and theme nights. These could include album release parties, tribute nights, or themed parties, providing diverse and exciting options for attendees.

Whether you're discovering a new favorite band, enjoying the live performance of a well-known artist, or immersing yourself in the local music scene, attending a concert at the Intersection is a dynamic and memorable experience. The venue's commitment to offering a diverse lineup ensures that there's always something for music enthusiasts of all tastes and preferences.

27.Explore the trails at Blandford Nature Center.

Exploring the trails at Blandford Nature Center in Grand Rapids offers a serene and immersive experience, allowing visitors to connect with nature, observe wildlife, and enjoy the peaceful beauty of West Michigan's natural landscapes. Blandford Nature Center, situated on over 140 acres, provides a network of well-maintained trails that wind through diverse ecosystems, making it an ideal destination for outdoor enthusiasts, hikers, and nature lovers.

Here's what you can expect when exploring the trails at Blandford Nature Center:

Trail System: Blandford Nature Center features a variety of trails that cater to different skill levels and preferences. Whether you're seeking a leisurely stroll, a brisk hike, or a more challenging trek, the trail system accommodates various outdoor activities.

Diverse Ecosystems: The trails meander through a range of ecosystems, including woodlands, wetlands, meadows, and fields. Each section offers unique flora and fauna, providing a rich tapestry of natural diversity for visitors to explore.

Wildlife Observation: Blandford Nature Center is home to a variety of wildlife species. As you traverse the trails, keep an eye out for birds, mammals, amphibians, and insects. The diverse habitats create opportunities for wildlife observation and birdwatching.

Educational Signage: Along the trails, you may encounter educational signage that provides information about the local flora, fauna, and ecological processes. These interpretive elements enhance the experience by offering insights into the natural world.

Scenic Overlooks: Some trails at Blandford Nature Center lead to scenic overlooks, allowing visitors to enjoy panoramic views of the surrounding landscapes. These vantage points provide peaceful spots for reflection and photography.

Seasonal Changes: The trails showcase the beauty of the changing seasons. From the vibrant colors of fall foliage to the blossoming flowers in spring, each season brings its own charm to the natural surroundings, creating a dynamic and ever-evolving outdoor experience.

Accessible Trails: Blandford Nature Center strives to make nature accessible to all visitors. Some trails are designed to be wheelchair-friendly, ensuring that individuals of all abilities can enjoy the natural beauty of the area.

Guided Programs and Events: The nature center often hosts guided programs, nature walks, and special events that provide additional opportunities for exploration and learning. Check the center's schedule for any organized activities during your visit.

Nature Center Facilities: In addition to the trails, Blandford Nature Center may have on-site facilities such as a visitor center, educational spaces, and rest areas. These facilities contribute to the overall visitor experience.

Whether you're looking for a peaceful nature walk, an invigorating hike, or a chance to engage in wildlife observation, the trails at Blandford Nature Center offer a rejuvenating escape within the city limits. It's a place where the beauty of the outdoors harmonizes with educational opportunities, providing a welcoming and accessible natural environment for individuals and families alike.

28. Visit the Grand Rapids African American Museum & Archives.

Visiting the Grand Rapids African American Museum & Archives (GRAAMA) is a culturally enriching experience that provides insight into the history, heritage, and contributions of African Americans in the Grand Rapids community. Located in the heart of the city, GRAAMA serves as a vital institution dedicated to preserving and sharing the stories of African Americans in West Michigan.

Here's what you can expect when visiting the Grand Rapids African American Museum & Archives:

Exhibits and Collections: GRAAMA features exhibits and collections that highlight the rich history and achievements of African Americans in Grand Rapids. The museum's displays may cover various themes, including local leaders, cultural milestones, and significant events that have shaped the African American experience in the region.

Archival Resources: As an archives center, GRAAMA houses a collection of historical documents, photographs, and artifacts that contribute to a comprehensive understanding of the African American history in West Michigan. Researchers and visitors alike can explore these archival resources to delve deeper into the stories of individuals and communities.

Educational Programs: GRAAMA is committed to education and community engagement. The museum often hosts educational programs, workshops, and events that promote a better understanding of African American culture, history, and contributions. These programs may be tailored for visitors of all ages.

Cultural Events: The museum may organize cultural events, celebrations, and gatherings that showcase the vibrancy of African American culture. These events provide an opportunity for the community to come together, celebrate heritage, and foster a sense of unity.

Community Outreach: GRAAMA is actively involved in community outreach efforts, collaborating with local schools, organizations, and community groups. This outreach helps promote awareness of African American history and culture and encourages participation from diverse segments of the community.

Historical Context: Through exhibits and interpretive displays, GRAAMA aims to provide historical context to the African American experience in Grand Rapids. This includes narratives of resilience, achievements, challenges, and contributions that have shaped the community over time.

Guided Tours: The museum may offer guided tours led by knowledgeable staff or docents. These tours provide visitors with a curated and informative experience, offering insights into specific exhibits and the broader historical context.

Gift Shop: Many museums have a gift shop where visitors can purchase books, art, and souvenirs related to African American history and culture. The gift shop at GRAAMA may offer a range of items that allow visitors to take a piece of the experience home with them.

Visiting GRAAMA is an opportunity to engage with the rich cultural tapestry of Grand Rapids and gain a deeper appreciation for the contributions of African Americans to the local community. It serves as a space for reflection, learning, and celebration of the diverse and impactful history of African Americans in West Michigan.

29.Attend the Festival of the Arts.

Attending the Festival of the Arts in Grand Rapids is a vibrant and festive experience that celebrates the rich cultural tapestry of the community. The Festival of the Arts is an annual event that brings together artists, performers, and community members to showcase and enjoy a diverse array of artistic expressions. Here's what you can expect when attending the Festival of the Arts:

Multidisciplinary Arts: The Festival of the Arts encompasses a wide range of artistic disciplines, including visual arts, performing arts, music, dance, theater, and more. The event serves as a showcase for the diverse talents of local and regional artists.

Outdoor Performances: The festival often features outdoor stages where live performances take place. From musical acts and dance troupes to theatrical performances, the outdoor venues create a lively and engaging atmosphere for attendees.

Visual Arts Exhibits: Explore visual arts exhibits that may include paintings, sculptures, photography, and other forms of visual expression. Many of these exhibits are set up in designated areas, allowing attendees to immerse themselves in the creativity of local artists.

Artisan Marketplace: The Festival of the Arts frequently includes an artisan marketplace where local artists and craftspeople showcase and sell their handmade creations. It's an excellent opportunity to discover unique and locally crafted artworks and goods.

Family-Friendly Activities: The festival is designed to be family-friendly, with activities catering to attendees of all ages. Children and families can enjoy interactive art projects, face painting, and other kid-friendly activities.

Culinary Delights: Indulge in a variety of culinary offerings from local food vendors. From traditional festival fare to unique and diverse food options, the culinary aspect of the festival adds to the overall sensory experience.

Parades and Processions: Some editions of the Festival of the Arts may feature parades or processions, adding a dynamic and colorful element to the event. These processions often involve community groups, performers, and artists showcasing their creativity.

Community Engagement: The festival encourages community engagement and participation. Attendees have the opportunity to interact with artists, learn about different art forms, and even contribute to collaborative art projects.

Live Demonstrations: Many artists participate in live demonstrations, providing insights into their creative process. This interactive element allows attendees to witness the artistic journey firsthand and engage with artists on a personal level.

Cultural Diversity: The Festival of the Arts embraces cultural diversity, featuring performances and exhibits that represent the rich tapestry of the Grand Rapids community. Attendees can experience and appreciate the cultural heritage of different groups within the region.

Music and Entertainment Stages: Multiple stages are set up to host a variety of musical acts and entertainment performances. These stages showcase local musicians, bands, and performers, contributing to the dynamic and celebratory atmosphere.

Attending the Festival of the Arts in Grand Rapids is not just an event; it's a community celebration that brings people together to appreciate, participate in, and enjoy the diverse and vibrant arts scene of the city. The festival typically takes place in the heart of downtown Grand Rapids and has become a beloved tradition that reflects the spirit and creativity of the local community.

30.Explore the Eastown neighborhood.

Exploring the Eastown neighborhood in Grand Rapids offers a charming and eclectic experience, characterized by its historic architecture, diverse community, and a vibrant mix of shops, restaurants, and cultural spaces. Here's what you can expect when exploring Eastown:

Historic Architecture: Eastown is known for its historic homes and architecture. Stroll through the tree-lined streets to admire a mix of well-preserved historic houses, including beautiful craftsman-style homes and early 20th-century architecture.

Unique Shops: Eastown is home to a variety of unique and independent shops. Explore boutique stores offering vintage clothing, handmade crafts, and eclectic goods. The neighborhood fosters a supportive environment for local businesses, contributing to a distinct and eclectic shopping experience.

Cafés and Coffee Shops: Enjoy the cozy and inviting atmosphere of Eastown's coffee shops and cafés. Whether you're looking for a quiet spot to work, relax with a book, or catch up with friends, the neighborhood offers a range of coffee destinations with character.

Local Eateries: Eastown boasts a diverse culinary scene, featuring a mix of locally owned restaurants serving a variety of cuisines. From trendy bistros to casual diners, you'll find options for every taste and budget.

Art Galleries: The neighborhood embraces the arts, and you may come across art galleries showcasing the works of local artists. These spaces contribute to the cultural richness of Eastown and offer a platform for the local art community.

Eastown Street Fair: If you visit during the annual Eastown Street Fair, you'll experience a lively event featuring live music, food vendors, art displays, and community engagement. The street fair is a celebration of the neighborhood's unique character and community spirit.

Community Events: Eastown hosts various community events throughout the year, ranging from neighborhood cleanups to music festivals. Check the local calendar to see if any events align with your visit.

Parks and Green Spaces: Enjoy the outdoors in Eastown's parks and green spaces. Wealthy Street Park, for example, provides a relaxing setting for picnics, casual sports, and community gatherings.

Live Music Venues: Eastown is home to live music venues where you can catch local bands and touring acts. These venues contribute to the neighborhood's vibrant nightlife and entertainment scene.

Community Murals: Admire vibrant murals adorning the walls of some buildings in Eastown. These murals often reflect the neighborhood's creative and artistic spirit, adding a colorful touch to the urban landscape.

Neighborhood Walkability: One of the charms of Eastown is its walkability. Explore the neighborhood on foot to fully appreciate its character, discover hidden gems, and engage with the friendly local community.

Diverse Community: Eastown is known for its inclusive and diverse community. The neighborhood attracts residents from various backgrounds, fostering a welcoming and open-minded atmosphere.

Whether you're interested in shopping for unique finds, savoring local cuisine, or simply enjoying the neighborhood's artistic and cultural offerings, exploring

Eastown provides a delightful and immersive experience in the heart of Grand Rapids.

31. Visit the Grand Rapids Civic Theatre.

Visiting the Grand Rapids Civic Theatre is a cultural treat that immerses you in the world of live performances, theatrical productions, and community engagement. Located in the heart of downtown Grand Rapids, the Civic Theatre has been a cornerstone of the city's arts scene for decades, providing entertainment and fostering a sense of community through the performing arts.

Here's what you can expect when visiting the Grand Rapids Civic Theatre:

Live Performances: The Civic Theatre stages a diverse range of live performances throughout the year. From classic plays and Broadway musicals to contemporary dramas and original productions, the theater's lineup caters to a wide audience with varied theatrical tastes.

Historic Venue: The Civic Theatre is housed in a historic building, adding to the charm and character of the overall experience. The venue itself may feature architectural elements that reflect its rich history in the Grand Rapids community.

Community Involvement: The Civic Theatre actively involves the community in its productions. This may include opportunities for local actors, directors, and behind-the-scenes contributors to participate in the creative process. The theater often collaborates with community groups, schools, and organizations.

Educational Programs: As part of its commitment to fostering a love for the performing arts, the Civic Theatre typically offers educational programs. These may include acting classes, workshops, and outreach initiatives designed to engage individuals of all ages in the world of theater.

Youth Programming: The Civic Theatre often features youth productions and programming, providing young aspiring actors with a platform to showcase their talents. These productions contribute to the development of young performers and create a family-friendly atmosphere.

Seasonal Lineup: The theater operates on a seasonal schedule, featuring a curated lineup of productions. Check the theater's schedule to see what shows are currently running or upcoming, ensuring you can plan your visit around a performance that interests you.

Cultural Events: In addition to regular productions, the Civic Theatre may host cultural events, fundraisers, and special performances. These events contribute to the theater's role as a cultural hub within the Grand Rapids community.

Accessible Venue: The Civic Theatre strives to be an accessible and inclusive venue. This includes efforts to accommodate patrons with varying needs and ensure that the magic of live theater is accessible to everyone.

Ticketing and Seating: Purchase tickets in advance to secure your seat for a performance. The theater typically offers various seating options, allowing you to choose the experience that best suits your preferences.

Supporting the Arts: Your visit to the Grand Rapids Civic Theatre not only provides entertainment but also supports the local arts community. The theater's role in fostering creativity, providing a platform for local talent, and contributing to the cultural fabric of Grand Rapids is integral to its impact.

Whether you're a seasoned theater enthusiast or someone exploring the performing arts for the first time, a visit to the Grand Rapids Civic Theatre promises an engaging and culturally enriching experience in the heart of the city.

32.Attend the Hispanic Festival.

Attending the Hispanic Festival in Grand Rapids is a vibrant and culturally rich experience that celebrates the diversity, traditions, and contributions of the Hispanic and Latino communities in West Michigan. The festival typically offers a lively atmosphere filled with music, dance, delicious cuisine, and various cultural activities. Here's what you can expect when attending the Hispanic Festival:

Cultural Performances: Enjoy a variety of cultural performances, including traditional dances, music, and live entertainment showcasing the rich heritage of Hispanic and Latino cultures. Performers often wear colorful costumes, and the music and dance reflect the diversity of Latin American traditions.

Live Music: Experience the rhythmic beats and melodies of Latin American music through live performances. From traditional folk music to contemporary Latin genres, the festival's musical lineup adds to the energetic and festive ambiance.

Culinary Delights: Explore a diverse array of Hispanic and Latino cuisine from different countries and regions. Food vendors at the festival offer a delicious selection of traditional dishes, providing an opportunity to savor authentic flavors.

Artisan Marketplace: The festival often features an artisan marketplace where you can browse and purchase handmade crafts, artwork, and traditional goods. This marketplace allows you to support local artisans and take home unique cultural items.

Family-Friendly Activities: The Hispanic Festival is designed to be family-friendly, with activities for all ages. Children can participate in games, arts and crafts, and cultural activities that provide a fun and educational experience.

Community Engagement: Engage with the local Hispanic and Latino community and learn about various organizations, businesses, and initiatives that contribute to the cultural fabric of Grand Rapids. The festival serves as a platform for community engagement and connection.

Educational Exhibits: Explore educational exhibits that highlight the history, traditions, and contributions of Hispanic and Latino communities. These exhibits may provide insights into the cultural diversity and heritage of different countries.

Parades and Processions: Some editions of the Hispanic Festival may feature parades or processions celebrating cultural pride. These colorful and lively processions often include traditional costumes, music, and dance.

Celebration of Heritage: Immerse yourself in the celebration of Hispanic and Latino heritage. The festival creates a welcoming and inclusive space where people from various backgrounds can come together to appreciate and celebrate the diversity within the community.

Dance Workshops: Participate in dance workshops or demonstrations that teach traditional Latin dances. It's an opportunity to learn new moves, enjoy the rhythm of Latin music, and embrace the joy of dancing.

Cultural Presentations: Attend cultural presentations, talks, or demonstrations that offer deeper insights into the customs, art, and traditions of the Hispanic and Latino cultures. These presentations provide a more comprehensive understanding of the community.

Community Unity: The Hispanic Festival fosters a sense of unity and pride within the Hispanic and Latino communities while also inviting people from all backgrounds to come together and celebrate the richness of diversity.

Attending the Hispanic Festival in Grand Rapids is a wonderful way to experience the warmth of the Hispanic and Latino cultures, enjoy lively festivities, and connect with the local community. It's an inclusive celebration that embraces the diversity that contributes to the cultural mosaic of West Michigan.

33.Take a scenic drive through Fallasburg Park.

Taking a scenic drive through Fallasburg Park in Grand Rapids promises a picturesque journey through nature, offering stunning views of the park's landscapes, historic covered bridge, and serene surroundings. Fallasburg Park is known for its natural beauty and provides a tranquil escape just a short drive from the city. Here's what you can expect on a scenic drive through Fallasburg Park:

Covered Bridge: One of the highlights of Fallasburg Park is the historic covered bridge. As you begin your drive, you'll likely cross this iconic structure, which adds a touch of charm to the scenic route. The covered bridge is not only a functional part of the park but also a picturesque feature that enhances the overall experience.

Rustic Roads: Fallasburg Park is often surrounded by rustic, tree-lined roads that provide a canopy of foliage, especially during the fall season. The changing colors of the leaves create a vibrant and visually stunning backdrop for your scenic drive.

Natural Beauty: The park is nestled along the Flat River, and your drive may offer glimpses of the water as well as the park's rolling hills and wooded areas.

The natural beauty of the landscape makes Fallasburg Park a serene and peaceful destination.

Wildlife Observation: Keep an eye out for wildlife as you drive through the park. Depending on the time of day and the season, you might spot birds, deer, and other creatures that inhabit the area. Fallasburg Park is known for providing a habitat for diverse wildlife.

Picnic Spots: The park offers designated picnic areas where you can stop, relax, and enjoy a meal surrounded by nature. Consider bringing a picnic basket to make the most of your scenic drive and take advantage of the park's inviting atmosphere.

Historic Ambiance: The park has a historic ambiance, with the covered bridge dating back to the 19th century. The combination of natural beauty and historical elements creates a unique and timeless atmosphere throughout your drive.

Hiking Trails: While on your drive, you may come across trailheads for hiking paths within the park. If you're interested in stretching your legs and exploring the area on foot, consider taking a hike along one of the scenic trails.

Seasonal Changes: Fallasburg Park exhibits a distinct beauty in each season. Whether it's the vibrant colors of autumn, the fresh greenery of spring, or the winter charm of snow-covered landscapes, the park transforms with the seasons, providing a different experience each time you visit.

Reflection Areas: Some areas within the park may offer reflective spots where you can pause and enjoy the tranquility of the surroundings. These spots often provide scenic views of the river or peaceful open spaces.

A scenic drive through Fallasburg Park is not just a journey through nature; it's an opportunity to unwind, appreciate the changing landscapes, and connect with the history and serenity that define this charming park near Grand Rapids.

34. Explore the Gaslight Village in East Grand Rapids.

Exploring Gaslight Village in East Grand Rapids offers a charming and vibrant experience, combining historic architecture, boutique shopping, delightful dining options, and a lively community atmosphere. Gaslight Village is known for its picturesque setting and is a popular destination for both locals and visitors. Here's what you can expect when exploring Gaslight Village:

Historic Architecture: Gaslight Village features well-preserved historic architecture that adds to its timeless charm. The streets are lined with historic buildings and tree-shaded sidewalks, creating a picturesque environment reminiscent of a classic American village.

Boutique Shopping: Enjoy a boutique shopping experience with a variety of specialty shops and boutiques. Explore unique stores offering clothing, home goods, accessories, and gifts. The emphasis on local businesses contributes to the distinctive character of Gaslight Village.

Cafés and Bakeries: Experience the cozy ambiance of local cafés and bakeries scattered throughout the village. These establishments often provide a perfect setting for a leisurely coffee, tea, or pastry while soaking in the village atmosphere.

Art Galleries: Gaslight Village may feature art galleries showcasing the work of local artists. Take a stroll through these galleries to appreciate the diverse artistry within the community.

Dining with a View: Enjoy dining at restaurants with outdoor seating that allows you to soak in the vibrant atmosphere of Gaslight Village. Many eateries offer a diverse range of culinary options, from casual fare to upscale dining.

Community Events: Gaslight Village often hosts community events, festivals, and gatherings. Check the local calendar to see if any events coincide with your visit. Community events contribute to the lively and inclusive spirit of the village.

Seasonal Decorations: Depending on the time of year, Gaslight Village may be adorned with seasonal decorations. Festive displays during holidays or seasonal changes enhance the overall charm of the village.

Walkable Streets: Gaslight Village is designed for pedestrian-friendly exploration. The walkable streets and well-maintained sidewalks invite visitors to leisurely stroll through the area, taking in the sights and sounds of the village.

Outdoor Seating Areas: Many establishments in Gaslight Village provide outdoor seating areas. Whether it's a café, restaurant, or ice cream shop, outdoor seating allows patrons to enjoy their meals or treats while savoring the village ambiance.

Local Events and Festivals: Gaslight Village is known for hosting local events and festivals that bring the community together. These events often include live music, art exhibits, and family-friendly activities.

Proximity to Reeds Lake: Gaslight Village is situated near Reeds Lake, providing an opportunity to extend your exploration to the scenic waterfront. Take a stroll along the lake, enjoy water activities, or simply relax by the shore.

Community Engagement: Gaslight Village fosters a strong sense of community engagement. The friendly atmosphere and local pride contribute to the welcoming environment that defines the village.

Whether you're interested in boutique shopping, savoring local cuisine, or simply enjoying the ambiance of a classic American village, Gaslight Village in East Grand Rapids offers a delightful and inviting experience.

35.Attend a comedy show at Dr. Grins Comedy Club.

Attending a comedy show at Dr. Grins Comedy Club in Grand Rapids promises an evening filled with laughter, entertainment, and the chance to enjoy performances from both established and emerging comedians. Dr. Grins, located inside The B.O.B. (Big Old Building) in downtown Grand Rapids, is a popular comedy venue known for its intimate setting and diverse lineup of comedic talent. Here's what you can expect when attending a comedy show at Dr. Grins:

Intimate Venue: Dr. Grins Comedy Club provides an intimate and cozy setting, creating an atmosphere where audience members can feel close to the comedians and fully engage with the performances. The club's design contributes to a shared experience of laughter among attendees.

Diverse Comedic Acts: The club features a diverse range of comedic acts, including stand-up comedians who bring various styles and perspectives to the stage. Whether you enjoy observational humor, storytelling, or witty improvisation, Dr. Grins strives to offer a mix of comedic styles to cater to different tastes.

Local and National Talent: Dr. Grins regularly hosts both local comedians and nationally touring acts. This combination allows audiences to discover new, up-and-coming talent while also enjoying the humor of established and well-known comedians.

Regular Show Schedule: Check the club's schedule for regular showtimes and upcoming events. Dr. Grins typically has a consistent lineup of performances, making it convenient for comedy enthusiasts to plan their visit and catch a show.

Bar and Refreshments: The venue often includes a bar where attendees can purchase refreshments, adding to the overall entertainment experience. Enjoy a drink while laughing along with the comedians on stage.

Comedy Special Events: In addition to regular shows, Dr. Grins may host special events, themed nights, or comedy festivals. These events provide unique and entertaining experiences for those seeking a bit of extra flair in their comedy outings.

Audience Interaction: Many comedians at Dr. Grins engage with the audience, creating moments of spontaneous and interactive humor. Be prepared for good-natured banter and a chance to become a part of the comedic experience.

Reservations: It's advisable to make reservations in advance, especially for popular shows. This ensures that you secure your spot and can enjoy the comedy performances without worrying about limited seating.

Post-Show Atmosphere: After the show, Dr. Grins and The B.O.B. offer an opportunity to extend the evening. Explore the vibrant downtown area, grab a post-show meal, or continue the entertainment with the various nightlife options nearby.

Attending a comedy show at Dr. Grins Comedy Club is a fantastic way to unwind, enjoy a night out with friends, and experience the humor of talented comedians. The intimate setting, diverse lineup, and lively atmosphere make it a go-to destination for those seeking laughter and entertainment in downtown Grand Rapids.

36.Take a horse-drawn carriage ride downtown.

Taking a horse-drawn carriage ride downtown in Grand Rapids provides a charming and leisurely way to explore the city's sights while enjoying a nostalgic and romantic experience. Whether you're looking for a special date night or a unique way to see the city, a horse-drawn carriage ride offers a delightful journey. Here's what you can expect on your downtown carriage ride:

Historic Downtown Setting: Your carriage ride will likely take you through the historic streets of downtown Grand Rapids, allowing you to appreciate the architecture and character of the city. Enjoy the ambiance of well-preserved buildings and landmarks.

Leisurely Pace: The carriage ride offers a leisurely pace, allowing you to relax and take in the scenery at a comfortable speed. This unhurried journey creates a serene atmosphere, perfect for enjoying the surroundings.

Professional Carriage Drivers: Your carriage will be guided by a professional and knowledgeable driver. Drivers often share interesting tidbits about the history and landmarks of the city, adding an educational element to your scenic ride.

Nostalgic Experience: Horse-drawn carriage rides evoke a sense of nostalgia and romanticism, providing a unique and memorable way to explore the city. The clip-clop of hooves and the gentle sway of the carriage contribute to the overall ambiance.

Customized Routes: Depending on the carriage service, you may have the option to choose a specific route or request stops at particular points of interest. This flexibility allows you to tailor the experience to your preferences.

Seasonal Decor: Depending on the time of year, your carriage ride may be accompanied by seasonal decorations. Festive lights during the holidays or blooming flowers in spring add an extra layer of charm to the experience.

Ideal for Special Occasions: A horse-drawn carriage ride is an ideal choice for special occasions such as anniversaries, proposals, or romantic evenings. The intimate setting and picturesque surroundings create a magical atmosphere.

Comfortable Seating: Carriages typically provide comfortable seating, often with cushions and blankets for added coziness. The goal is to ensure that passengers enjoy a relaxed and pleasant journey.

Evening Rides: Consider taking an evening carriage ride to experience downtown Grand Rapids under the soft glow of streetlights. The city takes on a different charm at night, offering a romantic and enchanting atmosphere.

Photographic Opportunities: Capture memorable moments during your carriage ride with the opportunity for unique and picturesque photos. The scenic beauty of downtown, combined with the carriage, creates a perfect backdrop for capturing the experience.

Before embarking on your horse-drawn carriage ride, it's recommended to check with local carriage services for availability, reservations, and any specific details about the route. Whether you're a visitor or a local resident, this nostalgic and leisurely journey through downtown Grand Rapids is sure to leave you with fond memories of the city's historic charm.

37.Explore the sculptures along the Grand Rapids African American Memorial Trail.

Exploring the sculptures along the Grand Rapids African American Memorial Trail provides a meaningful and visually engaging experience, showcasing art that commemorates the contributions, history, and culture of the African American community in the region. The trail is a testament to the rich heritage of the community and serves as a platform for artistic expression. Here's what you can expect when exploring the sculptures along the Grand Rapids African American Memorial Trail:

Monumental Sculptures: The trail features monumental sculptures that pay homage to significant figures, events, and themes within the African American experience. These sculptures are often strategically placed along the trail, creating a narrative that unfolds as you progress.

Historical Context: Each sculpture is designed to provide historical context and tell a story. The artists behind the sculptures may incorporate elements that symbolize resilience, unity, and cultural pride, offering viewers an opportunity to connect with the narratives embedded in the artwork.

Artistic Expression: The sculptures along the trail showcase a diverse range of artistic styles and expressions. From realistic portrayals to abstract forms, the artwork reflects the creativity and vision of the artists involved in bringing the memorial trail to life.

Interactive Installations: Some sculptures may incorporate interactive elements, allowing visitors to engage with the artwork on a more personal level. This interactivity enhances the overall experience, encouraging reflection and connection with the themes represented.

Cultural Significance: Each sculpture is deeply rooted in the cultural heritage of the African American community. The artists may draw inspiration from historical events, influential figures, and cultural traditions to create pieces that resonate with the community and its history.

Educational Components: Interpretive plaques or signage accompanying the sculptures provide educational insights into the significance of each artwork. These informational elements offer context, historical details, and explanations of the symbolism embedded in the sculptures.

Community Involvement: The creation of the African American Memorial Trail and its sculptures often involves community collaboration. Local artists, historians, and community members may have contributed to the development and realization of the trail, fostering a sense of ownership and pride within the community.

Scenic Surroundings: The trail itself is likely situated in a scenic location, providing a pleasant and contemplative environment for visitors. As you follow the trail, you may enjoy the natural surroundings, enhancing the overall experience.

Reflection Spaces: Some areas along the trail may include designated spaces for reflection. These spaces allow visitors to pause, absorb the meaning of the sculptures, and contemplate the narratives and themes presented.

Connection to Local History: The sculptures contribute to a broader understanding of local history, highlighting the role and impact of the African American community in shaping the identity of Grand Rapids. The trail serves as a dynamic and evolving testament to this history.

Before embarking on your exploration, consider checking with local authorities or organizations responsible for the trail to obtain information about guided tours, events, or any specific guidelines for visitors. Exploring the sculptures along the Grand Rapids African American Memorial Trail offers a unique and enlightening journey through art, history, and culture.

38. Attend a Grand Rapids Symphony performance.

Attending a Grand Rapids Symphony performance is a cultural treat that allows you to experience the beauty of live orchestral music in the vibrant arts scene of Grand Rapids. As one of Michigan's leading symphony orchestras, the Grand Rapids Symphony delivers captivating performances featuring talented musicians, renowned conductors, and a diverse repertoire. Here's what you can expect when attending a Grand Rapids Symphony performance:

World-Class Venue: Grand Rapids Symphony performances often take place in distinguished venues such as DeVos Performance Hall or other notable concert halls in the region. These venues provide an elegant and acoustically refined setting for a truly immersive musical experience.

Diverse Repertoire: The symphony's repertoire spans a wide range of musical genres, from classical masterpieces to contemporary compositions and popular pieces. This diversity ensures that there's something for every musical taste, making each performance a dynamic and enriching experience.

Acclaimed Musicians: The Grand Rapids Symphony boasts a talented ensemble of musicians who bring their expertise and passion to every performance. From string and wind sections to brass and percussion, the orchestra's skilled musicians contribute to the overall excellence of the musical presentations.

Guest Artists and Conductors: Depending on the program, you may have the opportunity to witness collaborations with world-renowned guest artists, including instrumental soloists, vocalists, and conductors. These collaborations bring an additional layer of artistry and excitement to the performances.

Seasonal Themes and Special Events: The symphony often organizes themed performances, seasonal concerts, and special events. These may include holiday celebrations, pops concerts, or thematic programs that add variety and thematic richness to the concert season.

Educational Initiatives: The Grand Rapids Symphony is actively engaged in educational initiatives, including programs for students, outreach to schools, and community engagement. Attending a performance may provide insights into the orchestra's commitment to music education and fostering a love for the arts.

Subscription Packages: Consider exploring subscription packages offered by the Grand Rapids Symphony. Subscribers often enjoy benefits such as discounted ticket prices, priority seating, and access to exclusive events, providing a more comprehensive and personalized concert experience.

Pre-Concert Talks and Events: Before some performances, the symphony may host pre-concert talks or events, providing additional context and insights into the pieces being performed. These sessions offer an opportunity to enhance your understanding and appreciation of the music.

Formal and Casual Attire: The dress code for symphony performances can vary, with some patrons opting for formal attire while others choose a more casual look. Check the specific recommendations for the performance you plan to attend, but most importantly, feel free to dress in a way that allows you to fully enjoy the experience.

Social and Cultural Experience: Attending a Grand Rapids Symphony performance is not only a musical event but also a social and cultural experience. It provides an opportunity to connect with fellow music enthusiasts, support the local arts community, and immerse yourself in the transformative power of live orchestral music.

Whether you're a seasoned classical music enthusiast or someone exploring the symphony for the first time, attending a Grand Rapids Symphony performance promises an evening of artistic excellence, emotional resonance, and the joy of experiencing live orchestral music in the heart of Grand Rapids.

39. Take a walk or bike ride along the White Pine Trail.

Taking a walk or bike ride along the White Pine Trail in Grand Rapids offers a scenic and recreational journey through nature, providing a tranquil escape from the urban environment. The White Pine Trail, stretching through Michigan, including parts of Grand Rapids, is a converted rail trail that offers a picturesque route for outdoor enthusiasts. Here's what you can expect during your walk or bike ride along the White Pine Trail:

Natural Beauty: The White Pine Trail is surrounded by natural beauty, featuring lush greenery, trees, and, in certain sections, views of rivers or streams. The trail allows you to immerse yourself in the serene landscapes and enjoy the changing scenery.

Converted Rail Trail: The trail follows the path of a former railroad line, providing a relatively flat and well-maintained surface for walking and biking. The conversion into a trail makes it accessible to people of various fitness levels and ages.

Scenic Views: As you traverse the trail, you may encounter scenic views, including open fields, wooded areas, and possibly wildlife. Keep an eye out for birds, squirrels, and other creatures that inhabit the natural surroundings.

Recreational Opportunities: The trail is suitable for both walking and biking, offering a recreational outlet for individuals, families, and outdoor enthusiasts. Whether you prefer a leisurely stroll or a more brisk bike ride, the White Pine Trail accommodates various activity levels.

Trailhead Access Points: The trail typically has designated trailhead access points where you can start your walk or bike ride. These access points may have parking facilities, informational signage, and amenities like benches or picnic areas.

Community Connections: The White Pine Trail often passes through or near communities, providing an opportunity to explore local neighborhoods, parks, and attractions along the way. Some sections may also have nearby amenities such as cafes or shops.

Seasonal Changes: Experience the trail's beauty in different seasons. Whether it's the vibrant colors of fall foliage, the fresh blooms of spring, or the peaceful snow-covered landscapes in winter, each season brings its own unique charm to the trail.

Family-Friendly: The trail is family-friendly, making it a great option for a day out with loved ones. Kids can enjoy the outdoors, and the relatively flat terrain makes it accessible for strollers or younger cyclists.

Exercise and Wellness: Walking or biking along the White Pine Trail provides an opportunity for exercise and wellness. It's a peaceful way to engage in physical activity, enjoy fresh air, and promote a healthy lifestyle.

Trail Etiquette: Be mindful of trail etiquette, such as yielding to other trail users, respecting nature, and following any posted guidelines. The trail is a shared space, and courtesy ensures a positive experience for everyone.

Trail Extensions: Depending on your preferences and available time, the White Pine Trail may connect to other trail systems or parks, allowing you to extend your outdoor adventure and explore more of the surrounding area.

Before embarking on your walk or bike ride, consider checking trail maps, local regulations, and any specific guidelines related to the section of the White Pine Trail you plan to explore. Whether you're seeking a leisurely stroll or an active bike ride, the White Pine Trail provides a scenic and rejuvenating escape into nature within the Grand Rapids area.

40. Visit the Voigt House Victorian Museum.

Visiting the Voigt House Victorian Museum in Grand Rapids is a step back in time, offering a glimpse into the elegance and lifestyle of the late 19th and early 20th centuries. The Voigt House, built in 1895, is a meticulously preserved Victorian-era home that showcases the opulence and design aesthetics of that period. Here's what you can expect when visiting the Voigt House Victorian Museum:

Historical Architecture: The Voigt House is a prime example of Victorian architecture, characterized by its intricate details, ornate facades, and distinctive features. Take a moment to appreciate the exterior design and craftsmanship of this well-preserved historic residence.

Guided Tours: Explore the interior of the Voigt House through guided tours led by knowledgeable docents. These tours provide insights into the history of the house, the Voigt family, and the broader societal context of the Victorian era in Grand Rapids.

Authentic Furnishings: The museum is furnished with authentic Victorian-era furniture, decor, and artifacts. Each room reflects the style and taste of the late 1800s, offering visitors a chance to experience the ambiance of a bygone era.

Period Rooms: The Voigt House features period rooms, each meticulously restored to capture the essence of different spaces within a Victorian household. Explore the living room, dining room, bedrooms, and other areas, each adorned with period-appropriate furnishings.

Cultural and Social Context: Gain a deeper understanding of the cultural and social context of the Victorian era in Grand Rapids. Learn about the lifestyles, societal norms, and technological advancements that influenced daily life during this period.

Gardens and Grounds: The Voigt House often includes well-maintained gardens and outdoor spaces. Take a stroll through the grounds to appreciate the landscaping and outdoor elements that complement the Victorian aesthetic.

Special Events and Programs: Check for special events and programs hosted by the Voigt House Victorian Museum. These may include lectures, workshops, or themed events that provide additional layers of engagement with Victorian history and culture.

Educational Opportunities: The museum serves as an educational resource, offering programs for schools and educational groups. It provides a hands-on learning experience for students and visitors interested in history, architecture, and the Victorian era.

Photography: Capture the beauty and historical significance of the Voigt House through photography. Some museums permit photography for personal use, allowing you to document your visit and share the Victorian charm with others.

Membership and Support: Consider becoming a member or supporting the museum through donations. Many historical museums rely on memberships and community support to continue their preservation efforts and educational programs.

Gift Shop: Explore the museum's gift shop for Victorian-themed souvenirs, books, and gifts. It's an opportunity to take home a memento that reflects the era you've experienced during your visit.

Before planning your visit, check the Voigt House Victorian Museum's official website for the latest information on operating hours, guided tours, special events, and any admission fees. Whether you have a passion for history, architecture, or simply appreciate the charm of Victorian homes, the Voigt House offers a delightful and immersive experience in the heart of Grand Rapids.

41.Explore local shops in the East Hills neighborhood.

Exploring the local shops in the East Hills neighborhood of Grand Rapids promises a diverse and eclectic shopping experience. Known for its vibrant and artistic atmosphere, East Hills is home to a variety of boutiques, galleries, and specialty stores. Here's what you can expect when exploring the local shops in East Hills:

Boutique Clothing Stores: Discover unique and stylish clothing boutiques offering a curated selection of apparel. From trendy fashion to vintage finds, East Hills has a range of shops catering to different tastes and styles.

Art Galleries: Explore art galleries showcasing the work of local artists. These galleries often feature a mix of paintings, sculptures, and other visual arts, providing an opportunity to immerse yourself in the local art scene.

Home Decor Shops: Find specialty stores offering a diverse range of home decor items. Whether you're looking for handmade crafts, vintage furniture, or contemporary design pieces, East Hills has shops that cater to interior design enthusiasts.

Bookstores: If you're a book lover, East Hills may have independent bookstores or shops with a carefully curated selection of books. Browse through the shelves to discover literary gems or unique publications.

Antique Shops: Uncover hidden treasures in antique shops that specialize in vintage and collectible items. These shops contribute to the neighborhood's charm by offering a glimpse into the past.

Local Artisan Markets: Look out for local artisan markets or pop-up shops that feature handmade goods crafted by local artisans. These markets often showcase one-of-a-kind items, including jewelry, textiles, and handmade skincare products.

Specialty Food Stores: Explore specialty food stores offering gourmet products, locally sourced ingredients, or unique culinary items. These shops contribute to the culinary diversity of East Hills and provide an opportunity to discover new flavors.

Thrift Stores: If you enjoy thrifting, East Hills may have thrift stores or secondhand shops where you can find pre-loved clothing, accessories, and home goods at affordable prices.

Craft Supply Shops: For those interested in DIY projects, check out craft supply stores that offer a variety of materials, tools, and inspiration for your creative endeavors.

Record Stores: If you're a music enthusiast, explore record stores that carry a selection of vinyl records, CDs, and other music-related merchandise. These stores contribute to the neighborhood's cultural vibe.

Jewelry Boutiques: Discover jewelry boutiques showcasing both contemporary and vintage pieces. Whether you're looking for statement pieces or delicate accessories, East Hills has options for jewelry enthusiasts.

Local Markets and Events: Keep an eye out for local markets or events that may feature a mix of vendors, artisans, and food stands. These events often bring a lively atmosphere to the neighborhood and provide an opportunity to support local businesses.

As you explore the local shops in East Hills, take the time to interact with shop owners, learn about the stories behind the products, and embrace the creative energy that defines this vibrant neighborhood. The eclectic mix of stores ensures that you'll find something special and unique during your shopping excursion.

42.Attend the Polish Festival.

Attending the Polish Festival in Grand Rapids promises a cultural celebration filled with traditional music, dance, delicious cuisine, and a vibrant showcase of Polish heritage. The festival typically offers a lively and immersive experience, allowing attendees to connect with Polish traditions and enjoy a sense of community. Here's what you can expect when attending the Polish Festival:

Cultural Performances: Immerse yourself in the rich cultural heritage of Poland through traditional performances. Enjoy vibrant folk dances, authentic music, and perhaps even participate in lively celebrations that showcase the diversity of Polish traditions.

Polish Cuisine: Indulge in a variety of mouthwatering Polish dishes and specialties. From pierogi (dumplings) and kielbasa (sausage) to golabki (stuffed cabbage rolls) and paczki (filled doughnuts), the festival is a culinary delight for those looking to savor authentic Polish flavors.

Art and Crafts: Explore displays of Polish arts and crafts, showcasing the creativity and craftsmanship of the culture. This may include traditional Polish pottery, embroidery, and other handmade items that reflect the country's artistic traditions.

Cultural Exhibits: Learn about Poland's history, traditions, and cultural significance through informative exhibits. Festivals often feature displays that provide insights into the country's rich heritage, allowing attendees to deepen their understanding of Polish culture.

Polish Beer and Beverages: Experience the flavors of Polish beverages, including Polish beer and other traditional drinks. The festival may feature beer gardens or tasting events where attendees can sample a variety of authentic brews.

Interactive Workshops: Engage in interactive workshops or demonstrations that showcase traditional Polish crafts, dances, or cultural practices. These hands-on experiences add an educational and participatory element to the festival.

Children's Activities: Festivals often include activities tailored for children, creating a family-friendly atmosphere. This may involve games, face painting, storytelling, or other entertainment options to keep younger attendees engaged.

Live Music and Entertainment: Enjoy live performances featuring Polish music, from traditional folk tunes to contemporary sounds. Festivals may host local and international musicians, creating a festive and energetic atmosphere.

Traditional Attire: Witness the beauty of Polish traditional attire, as festival attendees, performers, or even vendors may don traditional costumes that reflect regional styles and cultural significance.

Vendor Stalls: Explore vendor stalls offering a variety of Polish goods, souvenirs, and cultural items. This is an opportunity to purchase unique crafts, traditional clothing, and other items that showcase Polish craftsmanship.

Community Engagement: The Polish Festival fosters a sense of community and camaraderie. Attendees often have the chance to interact with members of the local Polish community, building connections and sharing in the festive spirit.

Parades and Processions: Some festivals feature parades or processions celebrating Polish heritage. These events may include colorful displays, traditional music, and participants showcasing their pride in their Polish roots.

Before attending, check the official festival website or local event listings for the latest information on dates, schedule, and any specific activities or performances. Attending the Polish Festival in Grand Rapids is a wonderful opportunity to celebrate the vibrant culture, traditions, and hospitality of the Polish community in a festive and welcoming environment.

43.Take a day trip to Lake Michigan's beaches.

Embarking on a day trip to Lake Michigan's beaches from Grand Rapids offers a refreshing escape to the stunning shores of one of the Great Lakes. With its sandy beaches, clear waters, and scenic landscapes, Lake Michigan provides an ideal setting for a day of relaxation and outdoor enjoyment. Here's what you can expect during your day trip:

Early Departure: Start your day trip early to make the most of your time at the beach. Lake Michigan's beaches are well worth the drive, and an early departure allows you to maximize your beach experience.

Travel to Grand Rapids Michigan

Choice of Beach: Lake Michigan boasts numerous beaches along its shoreline, each with its own unique charm. Popular options include Oval Beach in Saugatuck, Pere Marquette Beach in Muskegon, and Holland State Park Beach. Choose a beach based on your preferences and desired activities.

Scenic Drive: Enjoy a scenic drive from Grand Rapids to the chosen beach. The journey may take you through picturesque landscapes, charming towns, and scenic routes, offering glimpses of the beauty of western Michigan.

Beach Essentials: Pack beach essentials, including sunscreen, towels, beach chairs, umbrellas, and a cooler with snacks and refreshments. Comfortable clothing and swimwear are also essential for a day by the water.

Water Activities: Lake Michigan provides opportunities for various water activities. Depending on the beach, you can enjoy swimming, paddleboarding, kayaking, or simply wading in the clear waters. Check the conditions and any rental options available.

Relaxation: Unwind on the sandy shores of Lake Michigan. Whether you choose to stretch out with a good book, take a nap, or simply bask in the sun, the beach offers a tranquil environment for relaxation.

Picnic Lunch: Enjoy a picnic lunch with a view. Many Lake Michigan beaches have picnic areas or green spaces where you can savor your packed lunch while taking in the scenic surroundings.

Beach Walks: Take leisurely walks along the shoreline. The expansive beaches of Lake Michigan provide ample space for strolls, allowing you to enjoy the sound of waves, collect seashells, or simply take in the natural beauty.

Dune Exploration: Some beaches along Lake Michigan feature sand dunes. If applicable to your chosen beach, consider exploring the dunes for panoramic views of the lake and surrounding landscapes.

Sunset Viewing: If your schedule allows, stay until the evening to witness a Lake Michigan sunset. The sun setting over the vast expanse of the lake creates a breathtaking and memorable scene.

Local Eateries: Before heading back to Grand Rapids, explore local eateries in the beach town you visit. Some towns along Lake Michigan have charming cafes, seafood restaurants, or ice cream shops worth trying.

Evening Drive: Enjoy the scenic views once again as you drive back to Grand Rapids in the evening. The changing colors of the sky and the calming atmosphere contribute to a peaceful conclusion to your day trip.

Before your day trip, check the weather forecast, beach conditions, and any specific regulations or guidelines in place at the chosen beach. Whether you're seeking adventure, relaxation, or a bit of both, a day trip to Lake Michigan's beaches offers a memorable experience in the natural beauty of western Michigan.

44. Visit the Gerald R. Ford Boyhood Home.

Visiting the Gerald R. Ford Boyhood Home provides a unique opportunity to explore the early life and upbringing of the 38th President of the United States, Gerald R. Ford. The boyhood home, located in Grand Rapids, Michigan, offers a glimpse into the childhood and formative years of this influential political figure. Here's what you can expect during your visit:

Historic Setting: The Gerald R. Ford Boyhood Home is situated in a historic neighborhood in Grand Rapids. The surrounding area reflects the character of the time when Gerald Ford was growing up.

Guided Tours: Typically, guided tours are available to lead visitors through the various rooms of the boyhood home. Knowledgeable guides provide insights into Ford's early life, family history, and the cultural context of the period.

Authentic Interiors: The interiors of the boyhood home are preserved to reflect the time when Gerald Ford lived there. Explore the rooms where he spent his childhood, including the bedroom, living areas, and kitchen, to gain a sense of the family's daily life.

Family Artifacts: The home contains a collection of artifacts and memorabilia related to the Ford family. These may include personal items, photographs, and objects that provide a more intimate understanding of the family's history.

Educational Exhibits: In addition to the guided tour of the home, there may be educational exhibits on the premises. These exhibits often delve deeper into Gerald Ford's life, his achievements, and the historical events that shaped his presidency.

Gardens and Grounds: Some boyhood homes include well-maintained gardens and outdoor spaces. Take a stroll through the grounds to enjoy the surroundings and appreciate the exterior of the historic home.

Historical Context: Learn about the historical context of the time when Gerald Ford was growing up. Understand the societal changes, events, and influences that shaped his values and perspectives.

Visitor Center: The boyhood home may have a visitor center providing additional information, resources, and perhaps a gift shop where you can find souvenirs related to Gerald R. Ford.

Community Impact: Gain insights into Gerald Ford's connections to the local community. Learn about his early education, friendships, and the community values that played a role in shaping his character.

Presidential Legacy: The boyhood home is a part of Gerald Ford's larger presidential legacy. Explore how the experiences and lessons learned during his early years influenced his later career in politics.

Photography: Capture the experience with photographs, but be mindful of any restrictions on photography within the home. Many historic sites encourage visitors to document their visit for personal memories.

Before planning your visit, check the official website of the Gerald R. Ford Boyhood Home for the latest information on hours of operation, admission fees, and any special events or programs. Visiting the boyhood home is a meaningful way to connect with history and gain a deeper understanding of the person who would go on to become the President of the United States.

45. Explore the West Side neighborhood.

Exploring the West Side neighborhood of Grand Rapids offers a diverse and dynamic experience, characterized by a mix of historic charm, artistic vibrancy, and community engagement. Here's what you can expect when exploring the West Side:

Historic Architecture: The West Side boasts a rich history reflected in its architecture. Take a stroll through the neighborhood to admire historic homes, buildings, and landmarks that showcase the area's evolution over the years.

Bridge Street: Bridge Street is a central hub of activity on the West Side. This bustling street is lined with a variety of shops, restaurants, and cafes. Explore the local boutiques, galleries, and businesses that contribute to the neighborhood's unique character.

Public Art: The West Side is known for its vibrant public art scene. Look out for murals, sculptures, and other artistic installations that contribute to the neighborhood's creative atmosphere. These pieces often reflect the spirit and diversity of the community.

Local Breweries: Grand Rapids is renowned for its craft beer scene, and the West Side is no exception. Visit local breweries and taprooms to sample a variety of craft beers while enjoying the welcoming and relaxed atmosphere.

Riverside Park: Take a break in Riverside Park, a green space along the Grand River. The park offers scenic views, walking trails, and picnic areas, providing a tranquil retreat within the urban landscape.

Community Events: Check the local events calendar for community gatherings, festivals, and markets. The West Side often hosts events that bring residents together, fostering a strong sense of community.

John Ball Zoo: Located on the western edge of the West Side, John Ball Zoo is a family-friendly destination. Explore the zoo's exhibits, featuring a diverse array of animals, and enjoy educational programs and activities.

Local Eateries: Indulge in the culinary offerings of the West Side. The neighborhood is home to a variety of restaurants serving diverse cuisines, from trendy eateries to classic diners. Bridge Street Market is also a great spot for fresh and local groceries.

Neighborhood Parks: In addition to Riverside Park, explore other neighborhood parks and green spaces. These areas provide opportunities for outdoor activities, relaxation, and community gatherings.

Community Murals: Discover community-driven murals that tell stories and celebrate the cultural diversity of the West Side. These murals often reflect the collaborative efforts of local artists and residents.

Cultural Diversity: The West Side is known for its cultural diversity, which is evident in its businesses, events, and community initiatives. Embrace the multicultural atmosphere as you explore the neighborhood.

Heritage Hill Neighborhood: Adjacent to the West Side, Heritage Hill is a historic residential district known for its well-preserved homes. Take a self-guided walking tour to appreciate the architectural beauty of this neighborhood.

As you explore the West Side, consider engaging with local residents and business owners to gain a deeper understanding of the neighborhood's history, culture, and ongoing initiatives. Whether you're interested in art, history, or simply enjoying the local atmosphere, the West Side of Grand Rapids offers a rich and dynamic experience.

46.Go fishing at the Rogue River.

Embarking on a fishing excursion at the Rogue River in Grand Rapids provides a serene and nature-filled experience. Here's what you can expect and prepare for when planning a fishing trip to the Rogue River:

Fishing Regulations: Familiarize yourself with the fishing regulations and licensing requirements for the Rogue River. Ensure that you have the necessary permits to fish in the area, and adhere to any catch-and-release or size restrictions.

Fishing Gear: Pack your fishing gear, including a rod and reel suitable for river fishing. Consider the type of fish you intend to catch and bring appropriate bait, lures, and fishing line. Don't forget essential accessories such as tackle boxes, a landing net, and a cooler for any catches.

Fish Species: The Rogue River is home to various fish species, including trout and smallmouth bass. Research the seasonal patterns and preferences of the fish in the area to optimize your chances of a successful catch.

River Access Points: Identify suitable access points along the Rogue River where you can start your fishing expedition. Some areas may have designated fishing spots or public access points, ensuring you have the opportunity to explore different sections of the river.

Weather and Clothing: Check the weather forecast before your trip and dress accordingly. Wear comfortable, weather-appropriate clothing, including layered options. If you plan to wade into the river, bring suitable waders and footwear.

Fishing Etiquette: Respect other anglers and follow proper fishing etiquette. Keep a reasonable distance from fellow anglers, and avoid overcrowding popular fishing spots. Dispose of any trash responsibly and leave the environment as you found it.

Safety Measures: Prioritize safety during your fishing trip. If wading into the river, be aware of the water conditions and wear appropriate safety gear. Let someone know about your fishing plans and expected return time.

Nature Observation: Take the opportunity to observe the natural surroundings and wildlife along the Rogue River. The serene setting and the sounds of flowing water create a peaceful backdrop for your fishing adventure.

Fishing Techniques: Experiment with different fishing techniques based on the type of fish and river conditions. Whether you prefer fly fishing, casting, or trolling, adapt your approach to the specific characteristics of the Rogue River.

Catch and Release: If practicing catch-and-release, handle the fish with care to minimize stress and injury. Use barbless hooks, and release the fish back into the water promptly. Follow ethical angling practices to preserve the river's ecosystem.

Picnic and Relaxation: Pack a picnic lunch or snacks to enjoy during your fishing excursion. Many areas along the Rogue River offer scenic spots for a peaceful break, allowing you to relax and savor the natural beauty of the surroundings.

Fishing Guides: Consider hiring a local fishing guide who is familiar with the Rogue River. A guide can provide valuable insights, share expertise on local fishing conditions, and enhance your overall fishing experience.

Before heading to the Rogue River, check local fishing reports for the latest information on water conditions, fish activity, and any special considerations. With proper preparation, a fishing trip to the Rogue River can be a rewarding outdoor adventure surrounded by the beauty of nature.

47.Attend a poetry reading at the Literary Life Bookstore & More.

Attending a poetry reading at the Literary Life Bookstore & More in Grand Rapids promises an enriching and literary experience. Here's what you can expect during your visit to the bookstore for a poetry reading event:

Welcoming Atmosphere: Literary Life Bookstore & More likely provides a cozy and inviting atmosphere. The bookstore's setting creates an intimate space where poetry enthusiasts can gather to share and appreciate the written word.

Event Schedule: Check the bookstore's event schedule to find out when poetry readings or literary events, including author readings, are scheduled. Many bookstores host regular readings or feature local and visiting poets.

Diverse Poetic Voices: Poetry readings often feature a diverse range of poetic voices and styles. You may have the opportunity to listen to established poets, emerging talents, or even open mic sessions where local poets share their work.

Local and Visiting Poets: Literary Life Bookstore & More may host both local poets and visiting authors. This diversity allows you to explore a variety of perspectives and poetic forms, enriching your understanding of contemporary poetry.

Book Selection: Take the opportunity to browse and purchase poetry collections from the bookstore's selection. Many poetry readings include book signings, giving you the chance to have your copy signed by the author.

Q&A Sessions: Some poetry readings include Q&A sessions where the audience can engage with the poets, asking questions about their work, writing process, and inspirations. This interactive element enhances the overall experience.

Community Connection: Poetry readings at independent bookstores often foster a sense of community among attendees. You may have the chance to connect with fellow poetry enthusiasts, share insights, and discuss your favorite poems.

Literary Discussions: Following the readings, there may be opportunities for literary discussions or informal conversations about the poems presented. Engaging with others who share a passion for literature can be intellectually rewarding.

Intimate Setting: The intimate setting of a bookstore creates a unique environment for poetry readings. Unlike larger venues, you'll likely experience a more personal and close connection with the poets and their words.

Promotion of Local Talent: Bookstores like Literary Life often play a crucial role in promoting and supporting local literary talent. By attending poetry readings, you contribute to the vibrancy of the local literary scene.

Inspiration and Reflection: Poetry readings provide an opportunity for inspiration and reflection. The power of spoken word allows you to experience the nuances and emotions of a poem in a way that extends beyond the written page.

Event Calendar: Keep an eye on the bookstore's event calendar for upcoming poetry readings and other literary events. Many bookstores regularly update their calendars with diverse programming to cater to different literary interests.

Before attending, confirm the details of the poetry reading, including the featured poets, start time, and any registration requirements. Embrace the opportunity to immerse yourself in the world of poetry, surrounded by fellow literature enthusiasts, at the Literary Life Bookstore & More.

48.Explore the Creston neighborhood.

Exploring the Creston neighborhood in Grand Rapids offers a mix of historic charm, local businesses, and a sense of community. Here's what you can expect when wandering through Creston:

Cheshire Village: Start your exploration in Cheshire Village, a part of the Creston neighborhood known for its walkable streets, local shops, and diverse eateries. Explore the unique boutiques, cafes, and businesses that contribute to the neighborhood's character.

Local Cafes and Bakeries: Creston is home to several local cafes and bakeries. Take a moment to enjoy a cup of coffee or indulge in freshly baked treats while soaking in the neighborhood's atmosphere.

Diverse Architecture: Wander through Creston to appreciate the diverse architectural styles of homes and buildings. The neighborhood features a mix of historic residences and newer developments, providing a snapshot of Grand Rapids' evolving urban landscape.

Local Art Scene: Check out local art galleries or public art installations in Creston. Some areas may showcase murals, sculptures, or other artistic expressions that contribute to the neighborhood's creative spirit.

Creston Brewery: Visit Creston Brewery, a popular local spot known for its craft beers and a diverse menu. The brewery often serves as a gathering place for locals, offering a laid-back ambiance and a chance to enjoy live music.

Riverside Park: Explore Riverside Park, a green space along the Grand River. This park provides scenic views, walking trails, and recreational areas. It's a great place for a leisurely stroll or a relaxing afternoon outdoors.

Local Shops: Creston is home to a variety of local shops, including vintage stores, boutiques, and specialty shops. Take the time to browse and discover unique items that reflect the character of the neighborhood.

Creston Market: Check out Creston Market, a community-focused grocery store offering fresh produce, local products, and a friendly atmosphere. Supporting local businesses like this contributes to the neighborhood's sense of community.

Community Events: Stay informed about community events in Creston. The neighborhood may host events such as farmers' markets, street fairs, or festivals that bring residents together for shared experiences.

Neighborhood Parks: In addition to Riverside Park, explore other neighborhood parks in Creston. These green spaces provide opportunities for outdoor activities, picnics, and community gatherings.

Historical Sites: Learn about the history of Creston by visiting any historical sites or landmarks in the area. Some neighborhoods feature plaques or markers that provide insights into the local history.

Community Engagement: Engage with the local community by attending neighborhood meetings, participating in community initiatives, or connecting with local organizations. Creston's community spirit is strengthened through active involvement.

As you explore Creston, take the time to interact with residents, shop owners, and fellow explorers. Embrace the diverse and welcoming atmosphere of the neighborhood, and enjoy the blend of history, creativity, and community that defines Creston in Grand Rapids.

49.Take a scenic drive through the Fruit Ridge.

Embarking on a scenic drive through the Fruit Ridge in Grand Rapids offers a picturesque journey through orchards, farmlands, and rolling hills. Here's what you can expect and enjoy during your scenic drive:

Orchards and Fruit Farms: The Fruit Ridge is known for its orchards and fruit farms, producing a variety of fruits such as apples, peaches, cherries, and more. As you drive, you'll encounter vast orchards, especially during the fruit-bearing seasons.

Seasonal Blossoms: Depending on the time of year, you may be treated to the stunning sight of seasonal blossoms. Spring brings delicate blossoms to fruit trees, creating a vibrant and colorful landscape.

Country Roads: The drive through the Fruit Ridge often includes charming country roads that wind through the hills and valleys. These roads provide a peaceful and relaxing environment, perfect for a leisurely drive.

Scenic Overlooks: Look for scenic overlooks or designated viewpoints along the route. These spots offer panoramic views of the orchards, farmlands, and surrounding countryside, providing excellent photo opportunities.

Fall Foliage: In the autumn, the Fruit Ridge comes alive with vibrant fall foliage. The hills transform into a tapestry of reds, oranges, and yellows, creating a stunning display of seasonal beauty.

U-Pick Farms: Some fruit farms along the way may offer U-Pick experiences, allowing you to personally select and harvest your favorite fruits. Check in advance for any U-Pick opportunities and seasonal offerings.

Farm Markets: Explore farm markets or roadside stands that dot the Fruit Ridge. These markets often sell fresh, locally grown produce, baked goods, and artisanal products. It's a chance to taste and take home the flavors of the region.

Historic Barns: The countryside is often adorned with historic barns, adding to the rustic charm of the landscape. Take a moment to appreciate the architectural beauty and agricultural history of these structures.

Wildlife Observation: Keep an eye out for wildlife along the route. The rural setting of the Fruit Ridge provides habitat for various birds, deer, and other creatures. Bring binoculars for a closer look at the natural surroundings.

Country Estates: Some sections of the Fruit Ridge may include picturesque country estates or farmhouses. These properties contribute to the idyllic character of the landscape.

Local Vineyards: In addition to fruit orchards, you might encounter local vineyards producing wine. Consider stopping by a vineyard for a wine tasting experience and to enjoy the scenic views of vine-covered hills.

Relaxing Atmosphere: One of the highlights of a scenic drive through the Fruit Ridge is the overall relaxing atmosphere. The combination of nature, agriculture, and open spaces creates a serene environment, allowing you to unwind and appreciate the simple beauty of the countryside.

Before setting out, check for any seasonal events, road conditions, or specific points of interest along the route. Whether you're seeking a peaceful drive, a taste of local produce, or a connection with nature, the Fruit Ridge offers a delightful and scenic escape in the Grand Rapids area.

50.Attend a performance at Circle Theatre.

Attending a performance at Circle Theatre in Grand Rapids promises a captivating and immersive theatrical experience. Here's what you can expect during your visit to this vibrant community theater:

Diverse Productions: Circle Theatre is known for its diverse range of productions, including musicals, plays, and other theatrical performances. Check the theater's schedule to see what productions are currently running or upcoming.

Intimate Setting: Enjoy the intimate and cozy setting of Circle Theatre. The venue typically provides a close and engaging experience, allowing the audience to feel connected to the performers and the unfolding story.

Community Involvement: Circle Theatre is deeply rooted in community involvement. Many productions feature local talent, and the theater actively engages with the Grand Rapids community, fostering a sense of unity through the arts.

Musical Performances: If you attend a musical production, you can expect lively and dynamic musical performances. Circle Theatre often stages popular musicals, showcasing the talents of both actors and musicians.

Quality Acting: Experience high-quality acting from local and sometimes professional actors. Circle Theatre is committed to delivering performances that entertain and resonate with the audience.

Comfortable Seating: The theater typically provides comfortable seating, ensuring that the audience can relax and fully immerse themselves in the performance. Consider arriving early to choose preferred seating.

Historic Venue: Circle Theatre is housed in a historic building, adding character to the overall theater experience. The venue's history may contribute to the ambiance and charm of the space.

Seasonal Productions: Depending on the time of year, Circle Theatre may offer seasonal productions, such as holiday-themed shows or outdoor performances during warmer months. Check the schedule for seasonal highlights.

Accessible Location: Located in downtown Grand Rapids, Circle Theatre is conveniently accessible. Consider exploring nearby restaurants, cafes, or attractions before or after the performance to make the most of your visit.

Community Events: Keep an eye out for community events hosted by Circle Theatre. These events may include discussions, Q&A sessions with performers, or behind-the-scenes tours, providing a deeper understanding of the theater and its productions.

Ticket Information: Purchase tickets in advance to secure your spot for the desired performance. Circle Theatre typically offers various ticket options, including discounts for students or seniors.

Cultural Enrichment: Attending a performance at Circle Theatre contributes to the cultural richness of Grand Rapids. Immerse yourself in the arts, support local talent, and enjoy the unique and creative productions that the theater has to offer.

Whether you're a seasoned theatergoer or new to the world of live performances, Circle Theatre provides a welcoming and engaging space to enjoy the magic of the stage. Check the theater's website for the latest schedule and upcoming productions to plan your visit accordingly.

51.Explore the Alger Heights neighborhood.

Exploring the Alger Heights neighborhood in Grand Rapids offers a blend of historic charm, local businesses, and a tight-knit community. Here's what you can expect when wandering through Alger Heights:

Historic Architecture: Alger Heights is known for its charming historic architecture, including well-preserved homes and buildings that showcase the neighborhood's development over the years. Take a stroll through residential streets to admire the diverse architectural styles.

Local Businesses: The neighborhood is home to a variety of local businesses, including boutique shops, cafes, and restaurants. Explore Alger Heights to discover unique stores and establishments that contribute to the area's distinctive character.

Blanford Nature Center: While not directly in Alger Heights, the nearby Blanford Nature Center is worth a visit. This nature center offers trails, wildlife exhibits, and educational programs, providing a serene escape just a short distance away.

Community Events: Alger Heights hosts community events throughout the year. Check the local calendar for events such as street fairs, farmers' markets, or neighborhood gatherings, offering opportunities to connect with residents and experience the community spirit.

Alger Middle School: Explore the area around Alger Middle School, a local landmark that has been a part of the neighborhood's educational history. The school's presence may contribute to the sense of community in Alger Heights.

Green Spaces: Alger Heights features green spaces and parks where residents and visitors can relax. Enjoy a leisurely walk or find a quiet spot to read a book in one of the neighborhood parks.

Local Eateries: Alger Heights offers a range of dining options. Visit local eateries, cafes, or diners to experience the culinary offerings of the neighborhood. This is a great way to support local businesses and savor the flavors of the community.

Alger Heights Neighborhood Association: Engage with the Alger Heights Neighborhood Association to stay informed about local initiatives, events, and community news. This association plays a vital role in maintaining the neighborhood's identity and fostering a sense of belonging.

Seasonal Decorations: Alger Heights is known for its festive decorations during holidays, particularly during the Christmas season. Take a stroll during these times to enjoy the neighborhood's festive spirit and community-wide celebrations.

Library: Check out the local library in Alger Heights. Libraries often serve as community hubs, hosting events, book clubs, and providing resources for residents. It's a great place to connect with others who share a love for literature and learning.

Residential Gardens: Alger Heights residents often take pride in their gardens. As you explore the neighborhood, you may encounter well-tended gardens and front yards that add to the overall aesthetic appeal.

Friendly Atmosphere: One of the highlights of Alger Heights is its friendly atmosphere. The neighborhood's welcoming vibe makes it conducive to casual walks, meeting neighbors, and enjoying the sense of community that defines this area.

As you explore Alger Heights, take the time to interact with locals, visit the businesses, and appreciate the unique character that makes this neighborhood a distinctive part of Grand Rapids. Whether you're interested in history, local cuisine, or simply enjoying a stroll through a friendly community, Alger Heights has something to offer.

52.Attend the Festival of the Arts.

Attending the Festival of the Arts in Grand Rapids promises a vibrant and cultural experience, celebrating the arts in various forms. Here's what you can expect during your visit to this annual event:

Diverse Art Exhibits: The Festival of the Arts showcases a diverse array of art exhibits, featuring works by local and regional artists. Explore paintings, sculptures, photography, and other visual arts displayed in outdoor galleries and indoor spaces.

Live Performances: Enjoy live performances throughout the festival, including music, dance, theater, and more. Local performers and groups often take the stage, providing a dynamic and engaging atmosphere for festivalgoers.

Interactive Art Activities: Participate in interactive art activities and demonstrations. The festival often offers hands-on workshops, allowing attendees of all ages to create their own artwork and engage with different artistic mediums.

Street Performers: Be entertained by street performers showcasing their talents. From musicians and jugglers to magicians and living statues, the streets come alive with a variety of performances that add to the festival's lively atmosphere.

Culinary Delights: Explore a diverse range of food options from local vendors and food trucks. The festival is an excellent opportunity to indulge in a variety of cuisines while enjoying the outdoor ambiance.

Craft Market: Browse the craft market featuring handmade goods and artisanal products. Support local craftsmen and artisans by discovering unique and one-of-a-kind items.

Children's Activities: Bring the whole family, as the Festival of the Arts usually offers a range of activities for children. From arts and crafts to interactive games, there are plenty of kid-friendly options.

Community Involvement: The festival embodies a strong sense of community involvement. Local organizations, businesses, and artists come together to create a collective celebration of creativity and culture.

Parades and Processions: Some editions of the festival may include parades or processions, showcasing themed floats, costumes, and performances. Check the festival schedule for any planned parades during your visit.

Street Art and Murals: Explore temporary and permanent street art installations and murals created specifically for the festival. These artistic expressions add a visual dimension to the streets and contribute to the overall festive atmosphere.

Cultural Exhibits: Immerse yourself in the cultural richness of Grand Rapids through exhibits and displays that highlight the city's diverse heritage. Learn about local traditions, customs, and the cultural influences that shape the community.

Community Engagement: The Festival of the Arts is an excellent opportunity to engage with the local community. Connect with fellow attendees, artists, and volunteers, fostering a sense of unity and appreciation for the arts.

Before attending, check the festival's official website for the latest schedule, participating artists, and any additional details or special events. The Festival of the Arts is a highlight of Grand Rapids' cultural calendar, offering a festive and inclusive experience for all who appreciate creativity and artistic expression.

53. Visit the Van Andel Museum Center at the Public Museum.

Visiting the Van Andel Museum Center at the Public Museum in Grand Rapids promises an enriching and educational experience. Here's what you can expect during your visit to this cultural and historical institution:

Exhibits and Collections: Explore a wide range of exhibits and collections that cover various aspects of Grand Rapids' history, culture, and natural environment. The museum often features both permanent and rotating exhibits, providing a diverse and dynamic experience.

Grand Rapids History: Immerse yourself in the history of Grand Rapids, learning about the city's founding, growth, and key historical events. Exhibits may showcase artifacts, documents, and multimedia presentations that bring the local history to life.

Travel to Grand Rapids Michigan

Interactive Displays: The Van Andel Museum Center often incorporates interactive displays and hands-on exhibits, making the learning experience engaging and enjoyable for visitors of all ages. Interactive elements encourage exploration and discovery.

Native American Heritage: Discover exhibits that highlight the rich Native American heritage of the region. Learn about the indigenous peoples who have called the Grand Rapids area home and their contributions to the community.

Natural History: Explore exhibits on natural history, including displays of fossils, geological formations, and information about the region's unique ecosystems. Gain insights into the natural beauty and diversity of West Michigan.

Special Exhibitions: Check for any special exhibitions or temporary displays that may be featured during your visit. These exhibits often focus on specific themes, historical periods, or cultural topics.

Planetarium Shows: If the museum has a planetarium, consider attending a planetarium show. Learn about astronomy, space exploration, and celestial phenomena through immersive and educational presentations.

Architectural Beauty: Appreciate the architectural beauty of the Van Andel Museum Center itself. Many museums incorporate design elements that enhance the overall visitor experience, making the building a part of the cultural exploration.

Educational Programs: Check the museum's schedule for educational programs, workshops, and events. Some programs may be geared toward specific age groups or interests, providing additional opportunities for learning.

Family-Friendly Activities: The museum often offers family-friendly activities and programs, making it an ideal destination for visitors with children. Look for interactive zones designed to engage young learners.

Museum Store: Visit the museum store to browse a selection of books, educational toys, and souvenirs related to the exhibits. Purchasing items from the store can be a way to support the museum.

Visitor Information: Take advantage of visitor services, such as guided tours, maps, and information desks. Knowledgeable staff can provide insights, answer questions, and help you make the most of your museum experience.

Before your visit, check the museum's website for hours of operation, admission fees, and any special guidelines or events. The Van Andel Museum Center at the Public Museum in Grand Rapids offers a comprehensive and engaging exploration of the region's history, culture, and natural wonders.

54.Attend a workshop or class at the Grand Rapids Art Center.

Attending a workshop or class at the Grand Rapids Art Center offers a hands-on and creative experience. Here's what you can expect when participating in a workshop or class at this renowned art institution:

Diverse Art Classes: The Grand Rapids Art Center typically offers a variety of art classes and workshops, catering to various skill levels and interests. Explore options such as painting, drawing, sculpture, ceramics, photography, and more.

Experienced Instructors: Learn from experienced and knowledgeable instructors who are passionate about their craft. Instructors at the Grand Rapids Art Center are often artists themselves, bringing a wealth of expertise and creative insight to the classes.

Welcoming Environment: The art center provides a welcoming and supportive environment for participants of all skill levels. Whether you're a beginner or an experienced artist, you'll find a space where you can express yourself and enhance your artistic skills.

Hands-On Learning: Engage in hands-on learning experiences that allow you to actively create and experiment with different artistic techniques and mediums. Workshops may focus on specific projects or themes, providing a structured yet open-ended approach to creativity.

Access to Art Supplies: The Grand Rapids Art Center typically provides access to a variety of art supplies and materials needed for the workshops or classes. This ensures that participants can explore different mediums without the need to invest in extensive supplies.

Travel to Grand Rapids Michigan

Artistic Community: Connect with fellow participants who share a passion for the arts. Art classes at the center often foster a sense of community, encouraging collaboration, feedback, and the exchange of artistic ideas among participants.

Creative Exploration: The workshops and classes at the Grand Rapids Art Center encourage creative exploration. Whether you're discovering a new art form or honing existing skills, you have the opportunity to express yourself and push the boundaries of your creativity.

Gallery Exhibitions: Take advantage of the art center's gallery exhibitions, which may feature works by local and international artists. Gallery visits can complement your learning experience by exposing you to a diverse range of artistic styles and concepts.

Art Talks and Discussions: Some workshops or classes may include art talks, discussions, or critiques led by instructors or guest speakers. These sessions provide valuable insights and deepen your understanding of artistic concepts.

Portfolio Development: If you're pursuing art seriously, workshops at the Grand Rapids Art Center may offer opportunities for portfolio development. Instructors can provide guidance on building a cohesive body of work and refining your artistic voice.

Online Options: Depending on circumstances, the art center may offer online workshops, allowing you to participate from the comfort of your home. This flexibility can be especially beneficial for those with busy schedules or those living outside the immediate area.

Registration Information: Before attending a workshop or class, check the Grand Rapids Art Center's website for registration information, class schedules, and any prerequisites. Ensuring that you're well-prepared will enhance your overall experience.

Participating in a workshop or class at the Grand Rapids Art Center is not only an opportunity to learn and create but also a chance to immerse yourself in the vibrant and inspiring world of visual arts. Check the center's schedule, choose a class that aligns with your interests, and embark on a journey of artistic exploration and growth.

55.Go mountain biking at Merrell Trail.

Embarking on a mountain biking adventure at Merrell Trail in Grand Rapids promises an exhilarating experience surrounded by nature. Here's what you can expect during your mountain biking excursion at Merrell Trail:

Trail Overview: Merrell Trail is a popular mountain biking trail located in the Cannonsburg State Game Area, offering a mix of terrain suitable for riders of various skill levels. The trail system is well-maintained and designed to provide an enjoyable riding experience.

Trail Difficulty Levels: The trail typically features sections of varying difficulty levels, including beginner, intermediate, and advanced segments. This allows riders to choose routes that match their skill and comfort levels.

Scenic Surroundings: As you navigate the trail, you'll be surrounded by scenic natural landscapes. Merrell Trail takes riders through wooded areas, open fields, and along the Grand River, providing diverse and picturesque views.

Technical Features: The trail incorporates technical features such as berms, rollers, and jumps. These elements add excitement and challenge to the ride, making Merrell Trail suitable for both recreational and more experienced riders seeking thrills.

Trail Markings: Merrell Trail is typically well-marked with signs indicating trail difficulty, direction, and specific features. Pay attention to trail markings to ensure you follow the intended route and navigate safely.

Bike Rentals: If you don't have your own mountain bike, check if there are bike rental options available near Merrell Trail. Some local bike shops may offer rentals, allowing you to enjoy the trail without needing to bring your own bike.

Seasonal Considerations: Be mindful of seasonal conditions. While Merrell Trail is open year-round, factors such as weather, trail maintenance, and seasonal closures may impact the trail's accessibility. Check local trail conditions or the trail's official website for updates.

Safety Gear: Prioritize safety by wearing appropriate gear, including a helmet, gloves, and protective clothing. Mountain biking can be physically demanding, so ensure you're adequately equipped for a safe and enjoyable ride.

Trail Etiquette: Respect trail etiquette and be courteous to fellow riders and hikers. Follow established guidelines, yield to others when necessary, and maintain a responsible speed to enhance the overall trail experience for everyone.

Preparation: Before hitting the trail, ensure your mountain bike is in good condition. Check tire pressure, brakes, and other essential components. Bring water, snacks, and any necessary tools for basic bike maintenance.

Trail Connectivity: Merrell Trail may connect to other trail systems in the area. Explore the interconnected trails for a more extensive mountain biking adventure, discovering additional routes and scenery.

Post-Ride Relaxation: After an invigorating ride, take some time to relax and unwind. Consider bringing a picnic or finding a scenic spot near the trailhead to appreciate the natural surroundings.

Before heading to Merrell Trail, check for any trail updates, closures, or special considerations. By embracing the thrill of mountain biking at Merrell Trail, you'll have the opportunity to connect with nature, challenge yourself on diverse terrains, and enjoy the freedom of outdoor exploration.

56.Attend the Asian-Pacific Festival.

Attending the Asian-Pacific Festival in Grand Rapids promises a culturally rich and vibrant experience celebrating the diversity of Asian and Pacific Islander cultures. Here's what you can expect during your visit to this annual festival:

Cultural Performances: Enjoy captivating cultural performances showcasing traditional dances, music, and martial arts from various Asian and Pacific Islander cultures. These performances often provide a colorful and dynamic display of the region's artistic traditions.

Culinary Delights: Explore a diverse array of Asian and Pacific Islander cuisines. The festival typically features a variety of food stalls and vendors offering authentic dishes, allowing you to savor the flavors of different countries in the region.

Art and Craft Exhibits: Immerse yourself in the arts and crafts of Asia and the Pacific Islands. The festival may include exhibits showcasing traditional and contemporary artworks, handicrafts, and cultural artifacts.

Interactive Workshops: Participate in interactive workshops that provide hands-on experiences related to Asian and Pacific Islander arts and traditions. This could include activities such as traditional art forms, calligraphy, or cultural games.

Traditional Attire Displays: Admire the beauty of traditional attire from various Asian and Pacific Islander cultures. The festival often includes displays or fashion shows featuring traditional clothing, allowing attendees to learn about the significance of different garments.

Cultural Demonstrations: Witness live demonstrations of traditional practices, such as tea ceremonies, martial arts, or other cultural rituals. These demonstrations offer insights into the customs and heritage of the participating communities.

Marketplace: Explore a marketplace featuring vendors selling handmade crafts, cultural souvenirs, and unique items from Asia and the Pacific Islands. This provides an opportunity to purchase authentic and culturally significant products.

Educational Exhibits: Learn about the history, traditions, and contemporary issues of Asian and Pacific Islander communities through educational exhibits. These exhibits may highlight important cultural milestones, historical events, or community contributions.

Children's Activities: The festival often includes activities designed for children, allowing them to engage with and learn about Asian and Pacific Islander cultures in a fun and interactive way. This can include art projects, games, and storytelling sessions.

Community Engagement: The Asian-Pacific Festival fosters community engagement by bringing together people from various backgrounds. It's an opportunity to connect with members of the Asian and Pacific Islander communities, as well as individuals who share an interest in diverse cultures.

Traditional Music Performances: Enjoy traditional music performances that showcase the rich musical heritage of Asia and the Pacific Islands. This may include performances on traditional instruments, vocal ensembles, or contemporary fusion music.

Celebration of Diversity: Above all, the Asian-Pacific Festival is a celebration of diversity and unity. Attendees have the chance to appreciate and respect the unique cultures, languages, and traditions represented by the participating communities.

Before attending the festival, check the event's official website or local community announcements for information on schedules, featured performers, and any additional activities. By participating in the Asian-Pacific Festival, you'll have the opportunity to celebrate cultural diversity, build connections, and gain a deeper understanding of the rich tapestry of Asian and Pacific Islander cultures in Grand Rapids.

57.Explore the John Ball Park Zoo Wildlife Conservation Center.

John Ball Zoo is a popular attraction in Grand Rapids, Michigan, known for its commitment to education, conservation, and providing a fun and engaging experience for visitors.

Animal Exhibits: The zoo features a diverse range of animal exhibits, including mammals, birds, reptiles, and amphibians. Some notable exhibits may include big cats, primates, and a variety of species from different regions around the world.

Conservation Initiatives: Many modern zoos, including John Ball Zoo, actively participate in wildlife conservation efforts. This may involve supporting breeding programs for endangered species, habitat restoration projects, and educational programs to raise awareness about conservation issues.

Education Programs: John Ball Zoo offers educational programs and experiences for visitors of all ages. These programs aim to increase understanding about wildlife, conservation challenges, and the importance of biodiversity.

Interactive Experiences: The zoo may have interactive experiences for visitors, such as animal encounters, feeding opportunities, and behind-the-scenes tours. These activities provide a more immersive and educational visit.

Events and Special Programs: Throughout the year, the zoo hosts various events and special programs. These events often focus on conservation themes, allowing visitors to actively participate in and support wildlife conservation initiatives.

Wildlife Conservation Center (Hypothetical): If there is a specific "Wildlife Conservation Center" within John Ball Zoo, it could be a dedicated area or facility emphasizing conservation efforts. This might include information about ongoing projects, success stories, and ways visitors can contribute to conservation causes.

Membership and Support: Zoos often encourage visitors to become members, providing ongoing support for their conservation and education initiatives. Memberships may include perks such as free admission, discounts, and exclusive events.

Before planning a visit, it's advisable to check the official website of John Ball Zoo for the latest information on exhibits, conservation initiatives, and any new additions or changes. Additionally, you may want to inquire directly with the zoo about specific conservation centers or programs they may have developed since my last update.

58. Take a walk around Reed's Lake in East Grand Rapids.

Taking a walk around Reed's Lake in East Grand Rapids offers a picturesque and serene experience. Here's what you can expect during your stroll around this beautiful lake:

Scenic Views: Reed's Lake is known for its scenic beauty. As you walk along the shores, you'll be treated to tranquil views of the lake, surrounded by lush greenery and charming residential areas.

Walking Path: The lake features a well-maintained walking path that encircles its perimeter. This path provides a comfortable and scenic route for walkers, joggers, and cyclists to enjoy the outdoor surroundings.

Wildlife Watching: Keep an eye out for wildlife during your walk. Reed's Lake is home to various bird species, and you might spot ducks, geese, swans, and other waterfowl. The peaceful environment provides a habitat for local wildlife.

Boathouses and Docks: Along the shores of Reed's Lake, you'll likely encounter boathouses and docks. These picturesque structures add character to the lake's landscape and contribute to the overall charm of the area.

Seasonal Changes: The lake's beauty evolves with the seasons. In spring, you may witness blossoming flowers and trees, while autumn brings vibrant foliage. Each season offers a unique and visually appealing atmosphere.

Parks and Green Spaces: Reed's Lake is surrounded by parks and green spaces, providing additional areas to relax, have a picnic, or simply enjoy the outdoors. These spaces often have benches and open areas for recreation.

Residential Architecture: The neighborhoods around Reed's Lake showcase a mix of architectural styles, including charming cottages and grand homes. The walk offers glimpses of the local residential architecture, adding to the visual appeal.

Water Activities: While walking, you might see people engaging in various water activities on the lake. Kayaking, paddleboarding, and sailing are popular pastimes, adding to the vibrant and active atmosphere.

Cafes and Restaurants: Depending on the time of day, you might come across cafes or restaurants with lakefront views. Consider stopping for a refreshment or a meal to enhance your overall experience.

Community Atmosphere: Reed's Lake is often a hub for community activities. You might encounter local residents enjoying the outdoors, walking their dogs, or engaging in group activities, fostering a sense of community.

Fishing Spots: If you're interested in fishing, Reed's Lake provides opportunities for anglers. Check local regulations and, if applicable, bring your fishing gear to enjoy this relaxing pastime.

Sunsets: If you time your walk right, you can catch breathtaking sunsets over Reed's Lake. The changing colors reflecting on the water create a tranquil and visually stunning atmosphere.

Before heading out, check for any specific regulations or guidelines related to the use of the walking path and the lake area. Enjoy your leisurely walk around Reed's Lake, taking in the natural beauty and embracing the peaceful ambiance of this East Grand Rapids gem.

59. Visit the Grand Rapids African American Health Institute.

GRAAHI is a community-based organization dedicated to addressing health disparities and promoting health equity within the African American community in Grand Rapids.

Health Equity Initiatives: GRAAHI works on various health initiatives aimed at improving the overall well-being of African Americans. This includes addressing disparities in healthcare access, promoting healthy lifestyles, and advocating for policies that contribute to health equity.

Community Outreach and Education: The institute engages in community outreach and education efforts to raise awareness about health issues affecting the African American community. This involves organizing events, workshops, and providing resources to empower individuals to make informed health decisions.

Collaboration: GRAAHI collaborates with healthcare providers, community organizations, and other stakeholders to create a collective impact. By fostering partnerships, GRAAHI aims to implement effective strategies that lead to positive health outcomes.

Advocacy: GRAAHI advocates for policies and practices that eliminate health disparities and ensure equitable access to healthcare services. This includes addressing social determinants of health that contribute to disparities.

Research and Data Collection: GRAAHI may engage in research and data collection to understand the specific health needs of the African American community in Grand Rapids. This information informs their initiatives and helps tailor interventions to address specific challenges.

Health Promotion: The institute promotes healthy behaviors and lifestyles within the African American community. This may involve campaigns, workshops, and educational materials focused on preventing chronic diseases and improving overall health.

Cultural Competency Training: GRAAHI may provide cultural competency training for healthcare professionals to enhance their understanding of cultural nuances and improve the quality of care provided to African American patients.

Community Engagement: GRAAHI actively engages with the community through forums, events, and partnerships. This engagement ensures that the organization remains responsive to the evolving needs of the African American population in Grand Rapids.

60. Attend the Grand Rapids Balloon Festival.

Attending the Grand Rapids Balloon Festival promises a delightful experience filled with vibrant colors and the mesmerizing sight of hot air balloons taking to the sky. Here's what you can expect during your visit to this festival:

Hot Air Balloon Launches: The highlight of the Grand Rapids Balloon Festival is, of course, the hot air balloon launches. Witness the breathtaking moment as numerous colorful balloons ascend into the sky, creating a spectacular visual display.

Balloon Glow: Some balloon festivals include a "balloon glow" event in the evening. During a balloon glow, tethered balloons are illuminated in sync with music, creating a magical and enchanting atmosphere. It's a unique and captivating experience.

Balloon Rides: Depending on the festival, there may be opportunities for attendees to take hot air balloon rides. This provides a thrilling and scenic adventure, allowing you to see the surroundings from a completely different perspective.

Family-Friendly Activities: Balloon festivals often feature family-friendly activities such as games, face painting, and entertainment for children. It's a great event for families to enjoy together.

Food and Beverage Vendors: Explore a variety of food and beverage vendors offering a range of culinary delights. From festival classics to local favorites, you can indulge in delicious treats while enjoying the festivities.

Live Entertainment: Many balloon festivals include live entertainment, such as music performances, to enhance the overall atmosphere. Check the festival schedule for details on any scheduled performances.

Craft and Merchandise Vendors: Browse through craft and merchandise stalls offering unique items. This can be an excellent opportunity to find souvenirs or handmade goods from local artisans.

Photography Opportunities: The vibrant colors and unique shapes of the hot air balloons provide fantastic opportunities for photography. Capture the beauty of the balloons against the backdrop of the sky.

Community Engagement: Balloon festivals often bring the community together. Engage with fellow attendees, share the excitement, and enjoy the sense of camaraderie that comes with this joyful event.

Weather Considerations: Keep in mind that hot air balloon activities are weather-dependent. Events may be subject to change or cancellation due to adverse weather conditions, so it's advisable to check for updates before heading to the festival.

Parking and Transportation: Plan your transportation in advance and be aware of parking options. Some festivals may have designated parking areas, and it's a good idea to arrive early to secure a convenient spot.

Tickets and Admission: Check whether the festival requires tickets for entry and purchase them in advance if needed. Some balloon festivals offer free admission, while others may have a nominal fee.

To ensure a memorable experience, check the official website of the Grand Rapids Balloon Festival for the latest information, schedule, and any specific guidelines for attendees. Balloon festivals are magical events that offer a unique blend of visual beauty and community celebration.

61. Explore the Alpine Avenue shopping district.

Exploring the Alpine Avenue shopping district in Grand Rapids offers a diverse and vibrant retail experience. Here's what you can expect during your visit to this bustling shopping area:

Travel to Grand Rapids Michigan

Retail Variety: The Alpine Avenue shopping district is known for its diverse range of retail options. Explore a mix of stores, boutiques, and shops offering everything from clothing and accessories to home goods and electronics.

Big-Box Retailers: The district may feature prominent big-box retailers and department stores, providing a convenient one-stop shopping experience. These larger stores often offer a wide selection of products and brands.

Local Boutiques: Discover local boutiques and specialty shops that showcase unique and curated items. These smaller establishments may offer handmade crafts, locally designed fashion, and one-of-a-kind treasures.

Home Improvement Stores: If you're interested in home improvement or decor, the shopping district may include stores specializing in furniture, appliances, and home accessories. Explore the latest trends in interior design and find items to enhance your living space.

Electronics and Technology: Look for electronics and technology stores that cater to gadget enthusiasts. Whether you're in search of the latest gadgets or upgrading your tech gear, the district may have options for you.

Dining and Refreshments: Many shopping districts include cafes, restaurants, or food courts where you can take a break and enjoy a meal or refreshments. Consider trying a local eatery or grabbing a coffee to recharge during your shopping excursion.

Automotive Services: Depending on the area, you might find automotive services, including dealerships, accessory shops, and repair services. This can be convenient if you're in need of automotive-related products or services.

Shopping Centers and Malls: Explore shopping centers or malls within the district. These may house a collection of retailers, offering a comprehensive shopping experience with a variety of options.

Entertainment Options: Some shopping districts incorporate entertainment options such as cinemas, arcades, or entertainment complexes. Check for nearby attractions to complement your shopping experience.

Seasonal Events: Depending on the time of year, the shopping district may host seasonal events, sales, or festivals. Stay informed about any special promotions or activities taking place during your visit.

Accessibility: Consider the accessibility of the shopping district, including parking facilities and public transportation options. Well-planned districts often provide convenient and accessible transportation solutions for shoppers.

Community Atmosphere: Shopping districts often contribute to the local community atmosphere. Engage with friendly locals, explore the unique character of the area, and enjoy the sense of community that shopping districts can foster.

Before your visit, check online reviews, maps, and the official website of the Alpine Avenue shopping district for information on featured stores, events, and any special promotions. A well-planned exploration of the district can lead to exciting finds and an enjoyable shopping experience in Grand Rapids.

62.Attend the Diwali Festival of Lights.

Attending the Diwali Festival of Lights in Grand Rapids promises a vibrant and culturally rich experience. Here's what you can expect during your visit to this celebration of one of the most significant festivals in Hindu culture:

Traditional Decorations: Diwali, also known as the Festival of Lights, is characterized by colorful and elaborate decorations. Expect to see venues adorned with traditional lamps, candles, and vibrant rangoli (colorful patterns created on the ground).

Cultural Performances: Enjoy traditional music, dance, and performances that showcase the diversity of Indian culture. Performers may present classical dance forms, folk dances, and music that add to the festive atmosphere.

Diya Lighting Ceremony: A central ritual of Diwali is the lighting of diyas (oil lamps). Participate in or witness the ceremonial lighting of these lamps, symbolizing the victory of light over darkness and good over evil.

Fireworks Display: Diwali is often celebrated with fireworks to symbolize the victory of light and dispelling of darkness. Depending on the festival's location and regulations, there may be a fireworks display to mark the occasion.

Delicious Cuisine: Indulge in a variety of Indian delicacies and traditional sweets. Food stalls or vendors may offer a diverse range of dishes, providing a gastronomic journey through Indian cuisine.

Traditional Attire: Attendees often dress in traditional Indian attire during Diwali celebrations. Vibrant and elegant clothing, such as sarees and kurta-pajamas, adds to the festive atmosphere.

Candle-Lit Lanterns: In addition to diyas, decorative lanterns and candles are commonly used during Diwali. Look for displays of intricately crafted lanterns that contribute to the festival's luminous ambiance.

Puja and Religious Ceremonies: Diwali holds religious significance, and some events may include puja (worship) ceremonies. Participants gather for prayers, seeking blessings for prosperity and well-being.

Henna Art: Experience the intricate artistry of henna (mehndi). Many Diwali celebrations offer henna stalls where you can get temporary henna designs on your hands or other parts of the body.

Traditional Clothing and Jewelry Stalls: Explore stalls or shops that offer traditional Indian clothing, jewelry, and accessories. This can be an excellent opportunity to purchase or admire traditional items.

Cultural Exhibits: Some Diwali festivals include cultural exhibits that provide insights into Indian art, history, and traditions. Explore exhibits showcasing artifacts and information about the festival's cultural significance.

Community Unity: Diwali is a time for families and communities to come together. Embrace the sense of community unity, engage with fellow attendees, and learn more about the cultural diversity within Grand Rapids.

Before attending the Diwali Festival of Lights, check event details, schedules, and any specific guidelines on the official website or event announcements. Participating in Diwali celebrations offers not only a visually stunning experience but also a chance to appreciate the cultural richness and significance of this joyous festival.

63. Visit the Grand Rapids Public Library.

Visiting the Grand Rapids Public Library (GRPL) offers a chance to explore a hub of knowledge, resources, and community engagement. Here's what you can expect during your visit:

Architectural Beauty: The Grand Rapids Public Library is often housed in an architecturally significant building. Take a moment to appreciate the design and structure of the library, which may blend historical elements with modern functionality.

Vast Collection of Books: GRPL is home to an extensive collection of books covering a wide range of genres and topics. Whether you're interested in fiction, non-fiction, or specialized subjects, you're likely to find a diverse selection to explore.

Media and Audiovisual Resources: In addition to books, the library offers a variety of media resources. This may include DVDs, CDs, audiobooks, and digital resources, providing options for various learning and entertainment preferences.

Quiet Reading Areas: Enjoy a peaceful and serene reading environment in designated quiet areas. Many libraries provide comfortable seating and a conducive atmosphere for focused reading and study.

Digital Services: Explore the library's digital services, which may include e-books, online databases, and other digital resources. These services allow you to access information and literature from the comfort of your own device.

Children's Section: GRPL typically has a dedicated section for children, offering a colorful and engaging space for young readers. This area may include children's books, interactive displays, and storytelling events.

Community Events and Programs: Check the library's event calendar for community programs, book clubs, author talks, and other events. Many libraries actively engage with the community by hosting educational and entertaining programs.

Technology Access: Libraries often provide public computers and internet access. If you need to use a computer for research, job searches, or other tasks, the library may offer this service.

Reference Services: Take advantage of the library's reference services. Knowledgeable librarians can assist you in finding information, conducting research, and navigating the library's resources effectively.

Study Spaces: For students and researchers, libraries typically offer quiet study spaces. Whether you need to prepare for exams, work on a project, or engage in focused research, the library provides a conducive environment.

Art Exhibits: Some libraries feature art exhibits and displays. Check if the GRPL has any ongoing art exhibitions that you can explore during your visit.

Book Sales and Fundraisers: Libraries often organize book sales or fundraisers. Keep an eye out for these events, where you might find affordable books and support library initiatives.

64.Attend a River City Improv show.

Attending a River City Improv show in Grand Rapids promises an evening filled with laughter, spontaneity, and comedic creativity. Here's what you can expect during your visit to this improvisational comedy performance:

Interactive Comedy: River City Improv specializes in improv comedy, a form of entertainment where the content is created on the spot based on audience suggestions. The performers use their wit and quick thinking to craft humorous scenes, ensuring a unique and interactive experience.

Diverse Cast: The cast of River City Improv typically comprises talented and versatile comedians. Each member brings their own comedic style and energy to the stage, contributing to the dynamic and entertaining nature of the show.

Audience Participation: Improv thrives on audience participation. Be prepared to join in the fun by offering suggestions or even participating in on-the-spot games and sketches. The audience's input plays a crucial role in shaping the direction of the performance.

Spontaneity and Creativity: One of the key elements of improv is its spontaneity. The performers create scenes, characters, and narratives without scripts, relying on their creativity and collaboration to deliver hilarious and unexpected moments.

Family-Friendly Entertainment: River City Improv shows are often designed to be family-friendly, making them suitable for a wide range of audiences. It's a great option for a night out with friends, family, or even a date night.

Sketches and Games: The show may include a variety of improv games and sketches, each with its own set of rules and comedic objectives. From quick-fire word games to longer narrative sketches, the performance keeps the audience engaged with a diverse range of comedic formats.

Camaraderie and Chemistry: The chemistry among the performers is a crucial aspect of improv. The cast members work together seamlessly, building on each other's ideas and creating a sense of camaraderie that enhances the overall comedic experience.

Intimate Venue: Improv shows often take place in intimate venues, allowing for a close connection between the performers and the audience. The smaller setting creates an immersive experience where you can fully appreciate the spontaneity of the comedy.

Seasonal and Themed Shows: Depending on the time of year, River City Improv may offer seasonal or themed shows. These special performances can add an extra layer of humor and creativity to the improv experience.

Ticket Information: Check the River City Improv website or the venue's box office for ticket information, show schedules, and any special events. Purchasing tickets in advance is advisable, especially for popular performances.

65. Explore the Roosevelt Park neighborhood.

The Roosevelt Park neighborhood in Grand Rapids offers a diverse and vibrant community with a rich history. Here's an exploration of what you might find in this neighborhood:

Historical Significance: Roosevelt Park has historical significance, with roots dating back to the early 20th century. The neighborhood has evolved over time, reflecting the changing demographics and cultural dynamics of Grand Rapids.

Community Park: The neighborhood is home to Roosevelt Park, a central green space that serves as a hub for community activities. Parks often host events, picnics, and provide a place for residents to gather and socialize.

Cultural Diversity: Roosevelt Park is known for its cultural diversity, with a mix of residents from various backgrounds. This diversity contributes to a vibrant and inclusive community atmosphere.

Residential Architecture: Explore the residential streets to appreciate the variety of architectural styles in the neighborhood. You may find a mix of historic homes, mid-century designs, and more contemporary structures.

Local Businesses: Roosevelt Park may have local businesses, shops, and eateries that contribute to the neighborhood's character. Check out local establishments to get a sense of the community's commercial offerings.

Community Events: The neighborhood may host community events and gatherings throughout the year. These events could include festivals, parades, or cultural celebrations that bring residents together.

Schools and Educational Institutions: If you have an interest in education, explore local schools and educational institutions in the area. Neighborhoods often take pride in their schools, and these institutions contribute to the overall community identity.

Places of Worship: Roosevelt Park may have places of worship that are central to the community. These institutions often play a vital role in bringing people together for religious and community activities.

Public Art: Look for public art installations or murals that reflect the neighborhood's identity and values. Public art can add color and character to the streets, telling stories and capturing the spirit of the community.

Transportation Hubs: Consider the accessibility of the neighborhood. Proximity to public transportation hubs, major roads, and highways can be important factors in the overall livability of the area.

Civic Engagement: Roosevelt Park residents may actively participate in civic engagement and community organizations. Explore opportunities to get involved in local initiatives, neighborhood associations, or community improvement projects.

Outdoor Spaces: In addition to the central park, Roosevelt Park may have other outdoor spaces, such as playgrounds, walking trails, or sports facilities. These areas contribute to the recreational aspects of the neighborhood.

Before exploring Roosevelt Park, it's advisable to check local sources, community websites, or the city's official resources for any updates, events, or recent developments in the neighborhood. Engaging with local residents and community organizations can provide valuable insights into the unique character and offerings of Roosevelt Park in Grand Rapids.

66.Go birdwatching at Aman Park.

Birdwatching at Aman Park in Grand Rapids provides nature enthusiasts with an opportunity to observe a diverse range of bird species in a serene and natural setting. Here's what you can expect during your birdwatching adventure at Aman Park:

Varied Habitats: Aman Park encompasses diverse habitats, including woodlands, meadows, and wetlands. This variety attracts a wide array of bird species, making it an excellent location for birdwatching throughout the year.

Trails and Pathways: Explore the park's well-maintained trails and pathways. The network of trails takes you through different habitats, offering a chance to encounter birds in various settings. Keep your eyes and ears open for both woodland and open-area bird species.

Seasonal Birding: Different seasons bring different bird species to Aman Park. Spring and fall are particularly exciting times for migration, with many species passing through. Summer is ideal for observing breeding behaviors, while winter may bring opportunities to spot resident and migratory birds.

Woodland Birds: In the wooded areas, you might encounter songbirds such as warblers, thrushes, and woodpeckers. The forested sections provide a rich habitat for both resident and migratory species.

Meadow Birds: Open meadows within the park attract species that prefer grassy areas. Look for birds like sparrows, finches, and swallows in these open spaces.

Wetland Species: If Aman Park has wetland areas, these can be excellent spots for observing waterfowl, waders, and other wetland-associated birds. Check for ponds, marshy areas, or streams.

Birding Hotspots: Research or inquire about specific birding hotspots within Aman Park. Local birding guides or online resources may provide information on the best locations for spotting particular bird species.

Binoculars and Field Guide: Bring binoculars to get a closer look at birds from a distance. A field guide specific to the birds of Michigan can help you identify species you may encounter.

Patience and Quiet Observation: Birdwatching requires patience and a quiet approach. Take your time, move slowly, and listen for bird calls. Many birds are more active in the early morning, so an early start can be rewarding.

Respect Wildlife and Environment: Maintain a respectful distance from the birds to avoid disturbing them. Follow Leave No Trace principles, and be mindful of the natural environment.

Checklists and Apps: Consider using birdwatching checklists or mobile apps to keep track of the species you observe. Some apps can also provide real-time information on bird sightings in the area.

Weather Considerations: Be mindful of weather conditions, as bird activity can vary. Overcast days may encourage certain species to be more active, while sunny days can provide excellent lighting for observation.

Before your birdwatching excursion, check for any specific regulations or guidelines for birdwatching at Aman Park and familiarize yourself with the local birding community or groups that may share insights or organize birdwatching events in the area. Enjoy your birdwatching adventure at Aman Park, and may you encounter a diverse array of feathered friends along the way.

67.Attend a lecture or event at Grand Valley State University.

Attending a lecture or event at Grand Valley State University (GVSU) in Grand Rapids offers an opportunity to engage with academic and cultural activities. Here's what you can expect during your visit:

Event Calendar: Check the university's official website or event calendar for information on upcoming lectures, presentations, and events. GVSU hosts a variety of activities, including academic lectures, cultural events, and community discussions.

Diverse Topics: Lectures at GVSU cover a wide range of topics, reflecting the university's commitment to academic excellence and diversity. You might find talks on science, humanities, social issues, and more.

Guest Speakers: GVSU often invites distinguished guest speakers, scholars, and experts to share their insights. These speakers may come from various fields, providing a unique perspective on current issues or academic research.

Cultural and Arts Events: Explore events that showcase the cultural and artistic talents of the university community. This could include music performances, art exhibitions, theater productions, and more.

Community Engagement: GVSU is actively involved in community engagement, and some events may focus on community partnerships, service initiatives, and collaborative efforts with local organizations.

Educational Workshops: Look for educational workshops and seminars that cater to various interests. These sessions may offer opportunities for hands-on learning, skill development, and networking.

Student Presentations: Attend presentations or events featuring the work of GVSU students. This could include research presentations, creative projects, and performances showcasing the talents of the university's student body.

Public Forums: Some events may take the form of public forums or panel discussions, providing a platform for open dialogue on relevant issues. These discussions often encourage audience participation and engagement.

Networking Opportunities: Events at GVSU can be excellent networking opportunities. Connect with fellow attendees, faculty members, and students who share similar interests or professional goals.

Location and Facilities: Familiarize yourself with the specific location and facilities where the event will take place. GVSU's campus has modern facilities that contribute to a comfortable and engaging event experience.

Registration or Admission: Check if the event requires registration or admission. Some events may be open to the public, while others may have limited seating, so it's advisable to secure your spot in advance.

Check for Updates: Events may be subject to changes, so it's a good idea to check for updates closer to the date of the lecture or event. This ensures that you have the most current information.

Whether you're interested in academic discussions, cultural experiences, or community engagement, attending a lecture or event at Grand Valley State University can be a rewarding and intellectually stimulating experience. Plan your visit, explore the diverse offerings, and enjoy the vibrant atmosphere of the GVSU community.

68.Explore the West Michigan Whitecaps stadium.

Fifth Third Ballpark: The stadium itself, known as Fifth Third Ballpark, is the home of the West Michigan Whitecaps. It's located in Comstock Park, just north of Grand Rapids.

Minor League Baseball Experience: The West Michigan Whitecaps are a Class A-Advanced affiliate of the Detroit Tigers. Attending a game at their stadium offers a classic Minor League Baseball experience, with an emphasis on fun, entertainment, and affordable family-friendly outings.

Family Atmosphere: Minor League Baseball games are often known for their family-friendly atmosphere. Expect a welcoming environment with activities for kids, mascot appearances, and interactive games between innings.

Affordable Entertainment: Minor League Baseball games are usually more affordable than Major League Baseball games. Tickets, concessions, and merchandise are often priced reasonably, making it a cost-effective option for sports enthusiasts.

Promotional Nights: The West Michigan Whitecaps frequently host promotional nights and events. These could include themed nights, giveaways, or special activities to enhance the fan experience.

Concessions and Local Cuisine: Explore the variety of concessions available at the stadium. Many Minor League Baseball venues, including Fifth Third Ballpark, showcase local cuisine and signature dishes alongside traditional ballpark fare.

Scenic Views: Depending on your seat, you might enjoy scenic views of the surrounding area from the ballpark. Minor League stadiums are often designed to provide an intimate connection between fans and the game.

Mascot Interactions: The team's mascot, typically entertaining and lively, may make appearances throughout the game. This adds an element of fun and engagement, especially for younger fans.

Group Outings: The stadium offers options for group outings. Whether you're attending with friends, family, or colleagues, group packages may include special perks and seating arrangements.

Themed Nights and Events: Check the team's schedule for themed nights or special events. These could range from fireworks displays to tribute nights, adding extra excitement to the game.

Team Spirit and Merchandise: Immerse yourself in the team spirit by exploring the merchandise available at the stadium. Support the West Michigan Whitecaps with branded gear, hats, and jerseys.

Autograph Sessions: Depending on the schedule and player availability, there might be opportunities for autograph sessions. This can be a memorable experience, especially for fans looking to connect with the players.

Before planning your visit, check the West Michigan Whitecaps' official website for the latest schedule, promotions, and any updates. Enjoy the lively atmosphere, cheers of the crowd, and the thrill of baseball at Fifth Third Ballpark.

69.Attend the West Michigan Pet Expo.

Attending the West Michigan Pet Expo provides a delightful experience for pet enthusiasts and offers a platform to explore various aspects of pet care, products, and entertainment. Here's what you can expect during your visit to the expo:

Travel to Grand Rapids Michigan

Venue and Location: The West Michigan Pet Expo is likely held in a designated venue in the region. Check the event's official website or local announcements for details on the specific location and directions.

Exhibitor Booths: The expo typically features a variety of exhibitor booths showcasing pet-related products and services. Explore a diverse range of offerings, including pet supplies, accessories, grooming products, and more.

Pet Adoptions: Many pet expos, including this one, often collaborate with local animal shelters and rescue organizations. You may have the opportunity to meet adorable pets available for adoption, providing a chance to find your new furry friend.

Educational Workshops: Pet expos frequently host educational workshops and presentations. Attendees can learn about pet health, behavior, training tips, and the latest trends in the pet care industry.

Demonstrations: Enjoy live demonstrations featuring trained animals, showcasing their skills and entertaining the audience. These demonstrations may include agility courses, obedience training, and other impressive feats.

Meet-and-Greet with Vendors: Connect with pet product vendors, veterinarians, pet food specialists, and other experts in the industry. This provides a valuable opportunity to gather information, ask questions, and discover new products for your pets.

Pet Fashion Shows: Some pet expos feature entertaining pet fashion shows, displaying the latest trends in pet apparel and accessories. It's a fun and lighthearted aspect of the event.

Pet Photo Booths: Capture memorable moments with your pets at designated photo booths. These areas often provide props and backdrops, allowing you to create lasting memories with your furry companions.

Children's Activities: If the event is family-friendly, there may be activities tailored for children, such as face painting, pet-themed crafts, and interactive games.

Pet Health Screenings: Take advantage of any pet health screenings or consultations that may be offered. This can include basic health checks and advice from veterinary professionals.

Pet Contests: Participate in or enjoy pet contests that highlight the unique qualities and talents of various pets. Contests may include categories such as best costume, best trick, or cutest pet.

Networking with Fellow Pet Enthusiasts: The West Michigan Pet Expo is an excellent opportunity to connect with other pet owners and enthusiasts. Share experiences, exchange tips, and celebrate the joy of having pets in your life.

Before attending, check the official website of the West Michigan Pet Expo for event details, schedule, ticket information, and any specific guidelines. Whether you're a seasoned pet owner or considering bringing a pet into your life, the expo offers a delightful and informative experience for all attendees.

70.Explore the Belknap Lookout neighborhood.

The Belknap Lookout neighborhood in Grand Rapids is a historic and diverse area known for its elevated location, providing scenic views of the surrounding landscape. Here's an exploration of what you might find in the Belknap Lookout neighborhood:

Historic Charm: Belknap Lookout is characterized by its historic charm, featuring a mix of architectural styles that reflect the neighborhood's rich history. You'll find a blend of Victorian homes, mid-century structures, and more.

Elevated Views: As the name suggests, Belknap Lookout offers elevated views of the city. Take a stroll through the neighborhood, especially in areas with higher elevations, to enjoy panoramic views of Grand Rapids and the Grand River.

Medical Mile: The neighborhood is home to the Medical Mile, a prominent medical and research district that includes medical facilities, research institutions, and educational centers. This has contributed to the area's growth and development.

Heritage Hill Proximity: Belknap Lookout is adjacent to the Heritage Hill historic district, one of the largest urban historic districts in the country. Explore Heritage Hill to discover well-preserved Victorian homes and tree-lined streets.

Gerald R. Ford Presidential Museum: The Gerald R. Ford Presidential Museum is nearby, offering insights into the life and presidency of the 38th President of the United States. Explore exhibits, artifacts, and learn about the nation's history.

Grand Rapids Community College (GRCC): Belknap Lookout is close to Grand Rapids Community College, a higher education institution that has been an integral part of the community for decades.

Cultural Diversity: The neighborhood is known for its cultural diversity, with residents from various backgrounds contributing to the community's vibrant atmosphere.

Parks and Green Spaces: Explore local parks and green spaces for recreational activities. These areas may offer opportunities for outdoor relaxation, picnics, or simply enjoying the natural surroundings.

Local Businesses: Discover local businesses, cafes, and shops in the neighborhood. Belknap Lookout may have unique establishments that add to the community's character.

Access to the Grand River: Being in close proximity to the Grand River, residents and visitors can enjoy activities such as riverside walks, kayaking, or simply appreciating the scenic beauty along the riverbanks.

Community Engagement: Check for community events, neighborhood meetings, or initiatives that promote community engagement. Belknap Lookout residents often take an active role in shaping the neighborhood's identity.

Transportation Connections: Assess the neighborhood's accessibility and transportation options. Proximity to major roads and public transit can contribute to the overall convenience of living in or visiting Belknap Lookout.

Before exploring, consider checking local sources, community websites, or the city's official resources for any updates, events, or recent developments in the Belknap Lookout neighborhood. Engaging with local residents and community organizations can provide valuable insights into the unique character and offerings of this elevated and historically rich neighborhood in Grand Rapids.

71.Go rollerblading at Richmond Park.

Rollerblading at Richmond Park in Grand Rapids offers a scenic and recreational experience in a natural setting. Here's what you can expect during your rollerblading adventure at Richmond Park:

Trails and Pathways: Richmond Park features trails and pathways suitable for rollerblading. These paths wind through the park, providing a smooth surface for inline skating.

Natural Surroundings: Enjoy rollerblading amidst the natural beauty of the park. Richmond Park is known for its green spaces, mature trees, and peaceful ambiance, creating a refreshing backdrop for outdoor activities.

Lake Richmond: The park includes Lake Richmond, and you may find pathways around the lake suitable for rollerblading. Lakeside views can add a serene element to your skating experience.

Picnic Areas: Take advantage of the park's picnic areas. Consider bringing along a picnic and enjoy a relaxing break in the midst of your rollerblading session.

Wildlife Observation: Richmond Park is home to various wildlife, including birds and small animals. Keep an eye out for wildlife during your rollerblading excursion, adding a touch of nature to your outdoor adventure.

Fitness and Recreation: Rollerblading is an excellent form of exercise, and Richmond Park provides a spacious and scenic environment for fitness enthusiasts. Rollerblading is a great way to stay active while enjoying the outdoors.

Children's Play Areas: If you're rollerblading with family, Richmond Park typically has children's play areas. After your rollerblading session, children can enjoy playgrounds and recreational facilities.

Benches and Rest Areas: The park is equipped with benches and rest areas where you can take a break, enjoy the surroundings, or simply relax before continuing your rollerblading journey.

Seasonal Changes: Experience the park's beauty throughout the seasons. Rollerblading in spring and summer allows you to enjoy lush greenery, while fall brings vibrant foliage. Winter may offer a different experience if the park is suitable for winter sports.

Park Amenities: Check for park amenities, such as water fountains or restroom facilities, to ensure you have everything you need for a comfortable rollerblading outing.

Community Events: Depending on the time of year, Richmond Park may host community events or activities. Check local event calendars or park announcements for any special happenings during your visit.

Safety Precautions: Practice safety measures, including wearing appropriate protective gear such as helmets and pads. Be aware of park rules and etiquette to ensure a safe and enjoyable rollerblading experience for yourself and others.

Before heading to Richmond Park, it's advisable to check for any specific regulations, park hours, or updates. Enjoy the fresh air, the beauty of nature, and the exhilaration of rollerblading in this scenic park in Grand Rapids.

72.Attend the Polish Heritage Society Annual Dozynki Festival.

Attending the Polish Heritage Society Annual Dozynki Festival promises a rich cultural experience, celebrating Polish heritage and traditions. Here's what you can expect during your visit to this festival:

Cultural Celebrations: The Dozynki Festival is a cultural celebration that typically includes a variety of events, performances, and activities highlighting Polish traditions. Expect vibrant displays of Polish music, dance, and customs throughout the festival.

Traditional Polish Cuisine: Indulge in the rich and diverse flavors of traditional Polish cuisine. The festival is likely to feature a variety of authentic Polish dishes, allowing you to savor pierogi, kielbasa, golabki (stuffed cabbage), and other delightful treats.

Crafts and Artisans: Explore crafts and artisan booths showcasing Polish craftsmanship. You may find handmade items, traditional clothing, and unique artifacts that reflect the artistry of Polish culture.

Live Music and Dance Performances: Immerse yourself in the lively atmosphere with live music and dance performances. Polish folk music and traditional dances are often featured, providing entertainment that captures the spirit of the culture.

Dozynki Harvest Celebration: The Dozynki Festival traditionally marks the harvest season. The festival may include rituals and ceremonies associated with giving thanks for the harvest, often featuring beautifully decorated harvest wreaths.

Polish Folklore Displays: Learn about Polish folklore through exhibits and displays. This could include demonstrations of traditional crafts, storytelling, and explanations of symbolic elements embedded in Polish customs.

Family-Friendly Activities: The festival is likely to offer activities for families and children. Look for kid-friendly attractions, games, and educational experiences that make the event enjoyable for all ages.

Cultural Workshops: Participate in cultural workshops where you can learn about Polish traditions, language, or crafts. These hands-on activities provide an interactive way to engage with the cultural heritage.

Polish Merchandise: Explore booths selling Polish merchandise, including clothing, accessories, and souvenirs. It's an opportunity to take home a piece of Polish culture and support local artisans.

Community Engagement: The Dozynki Festival is a community event, providing a chance to engage with members of the Polish community and other festival-goers. Enjoy the welcoming and inclusive atmosphere.

Traditional Attire: Embrace the opportunity to wear or admire traditional Polish attire. Many attendees and performers may dress in traditional costumes, adding to the festive and authentic ambiance of the event.

Ceremonial Events: Look for any ceremonial events or religious observances that are part of the festival. These events may hold special significance within the Polish cultural context.

Before attending, check the official website of the Polish Heritage Society or local event listings for specific details, schedule, and any updates related to the Dozynki Festival. Enjoy a culturally enriching experience, celebrate Polish heritage, and partake in the festivities that make this annual event a cherished tradition in the community.

73.Explore the West Grand neighborhood.

Exploring the West Grand neighborhood in Grand Rapids offers a diverse and vibrant urban experience. Here's what you might discover during your exploration:

Local Businesses: West Grand is home to a variety of local businesses, including shops, cafes, and restaurants. Explore the neighborhood's unique offerings and support local establishments.

Cultural Diversity: The neighborhood is known for its cultural diversity, with residents from various backgrounds contributing to the vibrant atmosphere. Take the time to engage with the local community and appreciate the cultural richness.

West Leonard Business District: West Grand includes the West Leonard Business District, where you can find a mix of retail stores, eateries, and services. This district often hosts events and activities, creating a lively community hub.

Historic Architecture: Discover the charm of historic architecture in West Grand. The neighborhood features a mix of architectural styles, from classic homes to more modern structures.

Local Parks: Enjoy outdoor spaces and parks in the area. These green spaces provide opportunities for relaxation, picnics, and outdoor activities. Check out any local parks or recreational areas within West Grand.

Community Events: Stay informed about community events happening in West Grand. This could include neighborhood meetings, festivals, or cultural celebrations that bring residents together.

Street Art and Murals: Explore the streets to find vibrant street art and murals that contribute to the artistic character of the neighborhood. These public artworks often showcase local talent and add color to the urban landscape.

West Fulton Street: West Grand intersects with West Fulton Street, a major thoroughfare. Follow West Fulton Street to discover additional businesses, restaurants, and cultural attractions.

Community Organizations: West Grand may have active community organizations working on local initiatives and projects. Connect with these organizations to learn more about the neighborhood and get involved in community activities.

Schools and Educational Institutions: If you have an interest in education, explore local schools and educational institutions in the West Grand neighborhood. Schools often play a central role in community life.

Transportation Hubs: Assess the accessibility of the neighborhood. Proximity to major roads and public transportation hubs can be important for convenience and connectivity.

Local Landmarks: Look for local landmarks or points of interest in West Grand. These could include historic sites, public art installations, or buildings with unique significance.

Before your visit, check with local sources, community websites, or the city's official resources for any updates, events, or recent developments in the West Grand neighborhood. Engaging with local residents and community organizations can provide valuable insights into the unique character and offerings of this dynamic urban area in Grand Rapids.

74. Attend the Latinx Art Exhibition.

Attending a Latinx Art Exhibition in Grand Rapids promises a vibrant and culturally enriching experience. Here's what you can anticipate during your visit to such an exhibition:

Diverse Artworks: The Latinx Art Exhibition showcases a diverse range of artworks created by Latinx artists. Expect to see paintings, sculptures, photography, mixed media, and other forms of artistic expression.

Cultural Representations: Explore artworks that reflect the rich cultural heritage of the Latinx community. Artists often draw inspiration from their roots, traditions, and experiences, creating pieces that tell powerful stories.

Multimedia Presentations: Some exhibitions incorporate multimedia elements, such as video installations or digital art, providing a dynamic and immersive experience for attendees.

Community Engagement: Art exhibitions are often community-oriented events. Attendees have the opportunity to engage with artists, organizers, and fellow art enthusiasts, fostering a sense of community and cultural exchange.

Artist Talks and Panels: Many exhibitions include artist talks or panel discussions. These sessions offer insights into the creative process, inspirations, and the cultural significance of the artworks on display.

Live Performances: Some Latinx Art Exhibitions feature live performances, including music, dance, or spoken word poetry. These performances contribute to the overall celebration of Latinx culture.

Celebration of Identity: The exhibition may celebrate the diverse identities within the Latinx community. Artworks often explore themes of identity, immigration, heritage, and the intersectionality of being Latinx.

Local and Emerging Artists: Discover the work of both established and emerging Latinx artists. Exhibitions often provide a platform for emerging talents to showcase their creativity alongside more established figures.

Interactive Installations: Look for interactive installations that encourage audience participation. These installations may invite viewers to contribute to the artwork or engage in a sensory experience.

Art Market: Some exhibitions include an art market where attendees can purchase pieces directly from the artists. This is an excellent opportunity to support local talent and bring home unique artworks.

Thematic Focus: Exhibitions may have a specific thematic focus, addressing social issues, cultural preservation, or contemporary challenges faced by the Latinx community. These themes can add depth and meaning to the artworks.

Aesthetic Diversity: Appreciate the aesthetic diversity within the Latinx Art Exhibition. From traditional styles to contemporary expressions, the exhibition showcases the breadth of artistic approaches within the Latinx art scene.

Before attending, check the event details, schedule, and any associated programming on the exhibition's official website or local event listings. This ensures you make the most of your experience and gain a deeper understanding of the cultural narratives presented through the artworks. Enjoy the celebration of Latinx art, creativity, and cultural expression in Grand Rapids.

75.Visit the Friends of Grand Rapids Parks.

Visiting the Friends of Grand Rapids Parks offers an opportunity to engage with an organization dedicated to enhancing and preserving the city's green spaces. Here's what you might expect during your visit:

Mission and Values: Familiarize yourself with the mission and values of Friends of Grand Rapids Parks. This organization is likely committed to promoting, enhancing, and advocating for parks and public spaces in the community.

Visitor Center or Office: Check if Friends of Grand Rapids Parks has a visitor center or office. This could be a hub of information, providing details about their initiatives, ongoing projects, and ways for the community to get involved.

Educational Materials: Explore any educational materials available at their facility. This may include brochures, pamphlets, or displays that communicate the importance of parks, environmental conservation, and community engagement.

Volunteer Opportunities: Inquire about volunteer opportunities. Friends of Grand Rapids Parks often organizes community events and volunteer programs to maintain and beautify public spaces. Engaging in these activities allows you to contribute directly to the well-being of the community.

Park Advocacy Programs: Learn about park advocacy programs run by the organization. Friends of Grand Rapids Parks may be involved in advocating for policies that support green spaces and recreational areas.

Park Improvement Projects: Explore information about ongoing or upcoming park improvement projects. The organization may have initiatives to enhance infrastructure, accessibility, and amenities within the city's parks.

Community Engagement: Friends of Grand Rapids Parks likely fosters community engagement. Discover how they connect with residents, organize events, and collaborate with other community organizations to promote the value of parks.

Membership Opportunities: Check if there are membership opportunities available. Becoming a member may provide you with additional benefits, such as access to exclusive events, updates on park projects, and a sense of belonging to a community of park enthusiasts.

Events and Workshops: Inquire about any upcoming events or workshops hosted by Friends of Grand Rapids Parks. These events may cover topics related to environmental conservation, urban planning, or recreational activities.

Park Tours: If available, consider joining a park tour organized by the organization. This could be a guided tour highlighting the features, history, and significance of different parks in Grand Rapids.

Partnerships and Collaborations: Learn about partnerships and collaborations with other organizations, businesses, or government entities. Friends of Grand Rapids Parks may work closely with various stakeholders to achieve their goals.

Donations and Fundraising: Inquire about ways to support the organization through donations or fundraising efforts. This could involve contributing to specific projects, park maintenance, or general operational support.

Before your visit, check the organization's website or contact them directly to get the most accurate and up-to-date information. Friends of Grand Rapids Parks plays a crucial role in the community, and your visit can provide valuable insights into their efforts to create and maintain beautiful, accessible, and sustainable public spaces in Grand Rapids.

76.Explore the Midtown neighborhood.

Exploring the Midtown neighborhood in Grand Rapids promises a mix of cultural attractions, diverse businesses, and a lively urban atmosphere. Here's what you can discover during your visit to Midtown:

Cultural Institutions: Midtown is home to several cultural institutions and attractions. Explore the Grand Rapids African American Museum & Archives, which showcases the rich history and contributions of the African American community.

Medical Mile: Midtown is part of the Medical Mile, a prominent medical and research district in Grand Rapids. This area includes healthcare institutions, research facilities, and educational centers, contributing to the neighborhood's dynamic character.

Fulton Street Farmers Market: Experience the local flavors at the Fulton Street Farmers Market. This community market features fresh produce, artisanal goods, and a lively atmosphere. It's a great place to connect with local vendors and farmers.

Heritage Hill Historic District: Midtown is adjacent to the Heritage Hill Historic District, one of the largest urban historic districts in the United States. Take a stroll through Heritage Hill to admire well-preserved historic homes and architecture.

Local Businesses: Discover a variety of local businesses, including cafes, restaurants, boutiques, and shops. Midtown offers a diverse selection of places to explore, whether you're interested in culinary delights or unique retail finds.

East Hills Neighborhood: Midtown connects with the East Hills neighborhood, known for its artsy vibe and creative community. Explore local galleries, boutiques, and coffee shops in East Hills for a unique and eclectic experience.

Public Art and Murals: Midtown boasts vibrant street art and murals that contribute to the neighborhood's artistic flair. Take a self-guided tour to discover these colorful expressions adorning building exteriors and public spaces.

Community Events: Stay tuned for community events and festivals in Midtown. The neighborhood often hosts events that bring residents together, fostering a sense of community and celebration.

Local Parks: Enjoy outdoor spaces and parks within Midtown. These green areas provide opportunities for relaxation, picnics, and outdoor activities amidst the urban setting.

Entertainment Venues: Midtown may have entertainment venues, such as theaters or performance spaces. Check for upcoming shows, concerts, or cultural performances for an enjoyable night out.

Community Engagement: Engage with local community organizations and initiatives. Midtown residents often actively participate in neighborhood improvement projects, events, and community-building activities.

Transportation Hub: Assess the neighborhood's accessibility. Midtown's central location makes it well-connected to major roads and public transportation, providing convenient access for residents and visitors.

Before your visit, check local event calendars, community websites, or the city's official resources for any updates, events, or recent developments in the Midtown neighborhood. Whether you're interested in cultural exploration, culinary delights, or vibrant street life, Midtown offers a diverse and engaging urban experience in Grand Rapids.

77.Go horseback riding at Kent Trails.

Check Trail Regulations: Verify the latest trail regulations and usage policies for Kent Trails. Contact the local parks and recreation department or the managing entity responsible for the trail for the most current information.

Alternative Equestrian Trails: If Kent Trails does not permit horseback riding, inquire about nearby equestrian trails or parks that cater specifically to horse riders. Local equestrian facilities may offer guided rides or rental services.

Trail Conditions: Assess the trail conditions, especially if you plan to bring your own horse. Some trails may have specific requirements or restrictions based on weather conditions or maintenance activities.

Safety Precautions: Prioritize safety by wearing appropriate riding gear, including a helmet, and following any safety guidelines provided by trail authorities. Ensure that your horse is well-trained and accustomed to trail riding.

Local Stables and Rentals: If you don't own a horse, explore local stables or equestrian centers that offer horseback riding experiences. Some facilities may provide guided trail rides, lessons, or rental services.

Trail Etiquette: Familiarize yourself with trail etiquette for horseback riding. Be considerate of other trail users, follow posted guidelines, and practice responsible horsemanship.

Trail Maps: Obtain trail maps or information about the designated equestrian routes. This ensures that you stay on approved paths and avoid areas where horseback riding may be restricted.

Remember that conditions and regulations may change, so it's crucial to verify the current status of Kent Trails or any other trail you plan to explore for horseback riding. Local park authorities, trail managers, or equestrian organizations are valuable resources for obtaining the latest and most accurate information. Enjoy your horseback riding adventure in the beautiful surroundings of Grand Rapids!

78.Attend the Taste of Grand Rapids.

Attending the Taste of Grand Rapids promises a delightful experience filled with culinary delights and community spirit. Here's what you can expect during your visit to this popular food festival:

Culinary Diversity: The Taste of Grand Rapids showcases the diverse culinary scene of the city. Expect a wide array of food options representing different cuisines, cooking styles, and flavors.

Local Restaurants: Explore offerings from local restaurants and eateries. The festival often features a lineup of participating establishments, allowing you to sample signature dishes and specialties from some of Grand Rapids' best culinary destinations.

Food Tastings: Enjoy the main attraction – food tastings! The festival typically offers tasting portions of various dishes, allowing you to indulge in a variety of flavors without committing to full-sized meals.

Chef Demonstrations: Look for chef demonstrations and cooking shows. Renowned chefs may showcase their skills, share cooking tips, and engage with the audience, providing an entertaining and educational experience.

Beverage Tastings: Pair your food tastings with beverage options. Some festivals include beer or wine tastings, allowing you to discover local brews or wines that complement the diverse array of foods.

Live Entertainment: Immerse yourself in the festive atmosphere with live entertainment. Music performances, cultural displays, and other forms of entertainment contribute to the overall ambiance of the event.

Food Competitions: Some Taste of Grand Rapids events include food competitions or challenges. Watch chefs go head-to-head in friendly culinary battles, adding an exciting element to the festival.

Family-Friendly Activities: If the festival is family-friendly, expect activities for children. Face painting, games, and kid-friendly food options make the event enjoyable for the whole family.

Local Artisans and Vendors: Explore booths featuring local artisans and vendors. You may find unique crafts, food products, and culinary-related items that add to the overall festival experience.

Community Engagement: The Taste of Grand Rapids is a community event, providing an opportunity to engage with fellow residents, food enthusiasts, and local businesses. It's a great way to connect with the community and celebrate the city's culinary scene.

Outdoor Setting: Depending on the festival location, enjoy the outdoor setting. Open-air venues and outdoor seating areas create a pleasant environment to savor your food tastings and soak in the festive atmosphere.

Check Event Schedule: Prior to attending, check the event schedule for specific timings, performances, and special features. Planning your visit around specific events ensures you don't miss out on any highlights.

Before heading to the Taste of Grand Rapids, consider checking the festival's official website or contacting the event organizers for the latest information, ticket details, and any specific guidelines. Enjoy the gastronomic delights, cultural experiences, and community camaraderie that make the Taste of Grand Rapids a memorable and flavorful event.

79.Explore the Michigan Street Medical Mile.

Exploring the Michigan Street Medical Mile in Grand Rapids offers insights into a prominent healthcare and research district. Here's what you can discover during your visit to this significant area:

Healthcare Institutions: The Michigan Street Medical Mile is home to various healthcare institutions, medical centers, and hospitals. Prominent institutions include Spectrum Health, Van Andel Institute, and Mercy Health Saint Mary's.

Research Facilities: Explore research facilities and institutes dedicated to medical research and advancements. The Van Andel Institute, for example, is known for its contributions to biomedical research.

Medical Education: The area may host educational institutions specializing in medical and healthcare education. Check for medical schools or training programs associated with the healthcare institutions in the district.

Clinical Trials and Innovation: Learn about ongoing clinical trials and innovative healthcare practices. The Medical Mile often serves as a hub for cutting-edge medical research and the implementation of new technologies.

Health Sciences Center: Discover the Health Sciences Center, a hub for medical education, research, and clinical care. This facility may house classrooms, laboratories, and collaborative spaces for healthcare professionals.

Bioscience and Technology Companies: The district may also be home to bioscience and technology companies focused on healthcare innovations. These companies contribute to the development of medical devices, pharmaceuticals, and other healthcare solutions.

Public Art and Green Spaces: Explore public art installations and green spaces that add to the overall ambiance of the Medical Mile. Some areas may provide outdoor spaces for relaxation and reflection.

Walking Trails: The district may feature walking trails or pathways for pedestrians. These trails offer a convenient way to navigate the area while enjoying the surrounding urban landscape.

Medical Conferences and Events: Check for medical conferences, events, or symposiums hosted in the district. These gatherings bring together professionals, researchers, and experts from the healthcare field.

Community Engagement: Some institutions on the Medical Mile actively engage with the community. Look for outreach programs, educational events, or health fairs that promote community well-being and awareness.

Transportation Accessibility: Assess the accessibility of the district, including public transportation options and parking facilities. The Medical Mile's central location often provides convenient access for patients, visitors, and healthcare professionals.

Future Developments: Stay informed about any future developments or expansions in the Medical Mile. The district may undergo continuous growth and improvements, contributing to its status as a leading healthcare and research destination.

Before your visit, check with local authorities, the institutions in the area, or official district websites for any updates, guided tours, or specific points of interest. Exploring the Michigan Street Medical Mile provides a unique perspective on the intersection of healthcare, research, and education in Grand Rapids.

80. Attend the Lantern Launch at Robinette's Apple Haus & Winery.

Attending the Lantern Launch at Robinette's Apple Haus & Winery promises a magical and enchanting experience. Here's what you can expect during this captivating event:

Lantern Crafting: Before the launch, participants often have the opportunity to craft and decorate their lanterns. This hands-on activity adds a personal touch to the event, allowing individuals to express their creativity.

Community Gathering: The Lantern Launch brings together a community of people eager to share in the experience. It fosters a sense of unity and camaraderie as attendees come together to enjoy the festivities.

Evening Atmosphere: As the event takes place in the evening, you'll be immersed in a special atmosphere created by the glow of lanterns against the darkening sky. The twilight setting adds a touch of magic to the entire affair.

Scenic Venue: Robinette's Apple Haus & Winery provides a scenic and charming backdrop for the Lantern Launch. The picturesque surroundings contribute to the overall beauty of the event.

Live Entertainment: Some lantern launches include live entertainment, such as music or performances, to enhance the festive atmosphere. Check the event details for any scheduled performances.

Food and Beverages: Events at Robinette's often feature food and beverage options. Whether it's apple-themed treats, cider, or other delights, you can indulge in local flavors during the Lantern Launch.

Family-Friendly: The Lantern Launch is typically a family-friendly event, offering activities for children and a welcoming environment for people of all ages. It's an excellent opportunity for families to create lasting memories together.

Photography Opportunities: Capture the beauty of the lanterns taking flight against the night sky. The event provides fantastic photo opportunities, allowing you to document the magical moments.

Guidance and Safety Measures: Event organizers usually provide guidance on launching the lanterns safely. Follow any instructions provided to ensure a smooth and secure experience for all attendees.

Symbolic Meaning: Lantern launches often carry symbolic meaning, representing hopes, dreams, and positive intentions. Attendees may write messages or wishes on their lanterns before releasing them into the sky.

Environmental Considerations: Keep in mind any environmental considerations associated with lantern releases. Some events may use biodegradable lanterns or incorporate eco-friendly practices to minimize environmental impact.

Weather-Dependent: Note that outdoor events can be weather-dependent. Check the weather forecast and event updates to ensure a pleasant experience. Dress accordingly, especially if the evening tends to be cool.

Before attending the Lantern Launch at Robinette's Apple Haus & Winery, check the official event website or contact the venue for specific details, schedule, and any safety guidelines. Embrace the enchantment of watching lanterns illuminate the night sky in this special and memorable event.

81.Go rock climbing at Higher Ground Rock Climbing Centre.

Rock climbing at Higher Ground Rock Climbing Centre in Grand Rapids promises a thrilling and physically engaging experience. Here's what you can expect during your visit to this indoor rock climbing facility:

Variety of Climbing Walls: Higher Ground typically offers a variety of climbing walls suitable for climbers of all skill levels. Whether you're a beginner or an experienced climber, you'll find walls with different angles, holds, and challenges.

Safety Orientation: Before you begin climbing, you'll likely receive a safety orientation. This includes instructions on how to use the climbing equipment, safety measures, and guidelines for a secure climbing experience.

Climbing Equipment: The climbing facility provides the necessary equipment, including harnesses and climbing shoes. Staff members are available to assist you in properly fitting and using the equipment.

Bouldering Areas: In addition to roped climbing walls, Higher Ground may have designated bouldering areas. Bouldering involves climbing shorter walls without ropes, focusing on strength, technique, and problem-solving.

Instruction and Classes: If you're new to rock climbing or want to improve your skills, consider taking a climbing class or receiving instruction from experienced staff members. They can provide valuable tips on technique and safety.

Fitness and Fun: Rock climbing is not only a great physical workout but also a fun and engaging activity. It challenges both your strength and problem-solving abilities, making it an ideal fitness option for individuals seeking a dynamic workout.

Community Atmosphere: Indoor climbing centers often foster a sense of community. You'll likely encounter climbers of different skill levels, and the atmosphere is generally supportive and encouraging.

Youth Programs: Higher Ground may offer youth programs or climbing leagues for children and teenagers. These programs can introduce young climbers to the sport and provide a structured learning environment.

Event Nights: Some climbing centers host special event nights, such as themed climbs, competitions, or social gatherings. Check the facility's calendar for any upcoming events that may add an extra layer of excitement to your visit.

Pro Shop: The climbing center may have a pro shop where you can purchase climbing gear, accessories, and apparel. It's a convenient resource if you're looking to invest in your own climbing equipment.

Reservation System: Consider checking if the climbing center operates on a reservation system, especially during peak hours. Making a reservation ensures that you have dedicated climbing time and helps manage capacity.

Post-Climbing Relaxation: After your climbing session, you might find a lounge area where you can relax, chat with fellow climbers, or enjoy a refreshment. It's a chance to unwind and share your climbing experiences.

82.Attend the Grand Rapids Asian-Pacific Festival.

Attending the Grand Rapids Asian-Pacific Festival promises a culturally rich and vibrant experience celebrating the diverse heritage of Asian and Pacific Islander communities. Here's what you can expect during your visit to this cultural festival:

Cultural Performances: Enjoy captivating performances that showcase the diverse cultures of Asia and the Pacific Islands. This may include traditional dances, music, martial arts demonstrations, and other artistic expressions.

Traditional Cuisine: Indulge in a culinary journey with a variety of authentic Asian and Pacific Islander dishes. Food vendors may offer a wide range of delicacies, allowing you to savor flavors from different regions.

Art and Craft Exhibits: Explore art and craft exhibits featuring traditional and contemporary works from Asian and Pacific Islander artists. This provides an opportunity to appreciate the creativity and cultural expressions of the community.

Interactive Workshops: Participate in hands-on workshops and interactive activities that allow you to learn about traditional arts, crafts, or cultural practices. This engagement enhances the educational aspect of the festival.

Cultural Displays: Learn about the history, traditions, and customs of various Asian and Pacific Islander cultures through informative displays. Cultural booths may provide insights into heritage, attire, and significant cultural elements.

Fashion Shows: Experience the beauty and diversity of traditional and modern Asian-Pacific fashion through vibrant fashion shows. These showcases often feature clothing styles from different countries within the region.

Community Engagement: The festival fosters community engagement, providing an opportunity to connect with members of the Asian and Pacific Islander communities in Grand Rapids. Engage in conversations, make new friends, and build cultural understanding.

Children's Activities: Family-friendly activities are often a part of the festival, catering to children with games, crafts, and educational experiences. It's a family-oriented event that encourages intergenerational participation.

Cultural Competitions: Some festivals may host cultural competitions, such as traditional dance contests or martial arts demonstrations. These events add a competitive and entertaining element to the celebration.

Asian-Pacific Market: Explore a marketplace showcasing unique products, crafts, and goods from Asia and the Pacific Islands. It's an excellent opportunity to purchase souvenirs and support local vendors.

Community Performances: Besides professional performances, community groups and individuals may also showcase their talents. This adds a grassroots and community-driven dimension to the festival.

Symbolic Ceremonies: Witness symbolic ceremonies or rituals that hold cultural significance for participating communities. These ceremonies may mark the beginning or culmination of specific festival activities.

Before attending the Grand Rapids Asian-Pacific Festival, check the event's official website or contact the organizers for detailed information on the schedule, participating performers, and any additional attractions. Embrace the

cultural diversity, artistic expressions, and community spirit that make the
Asian-Pacific Festival a vibrant and inclusive celebration in Grand Rapids.

83.Explore the Madison Square neighborhood.

Exploring the Madison Square neighborhood in Grand Rapids offers a glimpse
into a diverse and historic community. Here's what you can discover during your
visit to this vibrant neighborhood:

Historical Architecture: Madison Square is known for its historic architecture,
featuring a mix of residential and commercial buildings. Take a stroll through
the streets to admire the unique designs and styles that reflect the neighborhood's
history.

Local Businesses: Explore the local businesses that line the streets of Madison
Square. From small shops to family-owned restaurants, the neighborhood offers
a variety of places to shop, dine, and support local entrepreneurs.

Community Parks: Enjoy outdoor spaces and community parks within Madison
Square. These green areas provide residents and visitors with places to relax,
play, and connect with nature.

Cultural Diversity: Madison Square is home to a diverse community, with
residents representing various cultural backgrounds. Embrace the multicultural
atmosphere and engage with the local community to learn more about its rich
diversity.

Artistic Expressions: Look for murals, street art, and other artistic expressions
that contribute to the creative atmosphere of the neighborhood. Public art
projects may showcase the talents of local artists and add vibrancy to the streets.

Local Events: Check for local events and community gatherings happening in
Madison Square. The neighborhood may host festivals, markets, or cultural
celebrations that bring residents together for shared experiences.

Historic Sites: Explore any historic sites or landmarks in the area. Madison
Square may have buildings or locations with historical significance that provide
insights into the neighborhood's past.

Community Centers: Visit community centers or gathering spaces that serve as hubs for residents. These centers may host educational programs, recreational activities, and events that strengthen community bonds.

Local Eateries: Indulge in the culinary offerings of Madison Square. From cozy cafes to ethnic restaurants, the neighborhood is likely to have a diverse array of dining options to satisfy various tastes.

Neighborhood Associations: Learn about local neighborhood associations that work to enhance the quality of life in Madison Square. These associations often organize community initiatives, improvement projects, and advocacy efforts.

Public Services: Familiarize yourself with public services available in the neighborhood, such as schools, libraries, and healthcare facilities. Madison Square aims to provide essential services for its residents.

Transportation Accessibility: Assess the accessibility of Madison Square in terms of public transportation and roadways. Understanding the transportation options helps you navigate the neighborhood efficiently.

Before your visit, check with local sources, community websites, or neighborhood associations for any upcoming events, initiatives, or developments in Madison Square. Exploring this dynamic neighborhood allows you to connect with the local community, appreciate its cultural richness, and discover the unique charm that defines Madison Square in Grand Rapids.

84.Go zip-lining at Cannonsburg Ski Area.

Embarking on a zip-lining adventure at Cannonsburg Ski Area in Grand Rapids offers a unique and exhilarating experience set against the picturesque backdrop of Michigan's natural beauty. Cannonsburg, traditionally known for its winter sports, transforms into a thrilling destination during the warmer months, providing an exciting zip-lining course that allows participants to soar through the treetops.

As you gear up for this adventure, you'll find yourself surrounded by lush greenery, offering a stark contrast to the snowy landscapes typically associated with Cannonsburg. The zip lines are strategically designed to traverse the terrain, providing not only an adrenaline-pumping journey but also breathtaking panoramic views of the surrounding landscape.

Navigating the zip lines at Cannonsburg Ski Area is not just about the thrill of speed; it's a journey that immerses you in the serene beauty of the Michigan outdoors. The courses are often carefully integrated into the natural environment, allowing participants to connect with nature while experiencing the excitement of zip-lining.

Safety is paramount in such endeavors, and Cannonsburg Ski Area typically prioritizes a comprehensive safety protocol. Before embarking on your zip-lining adventure, you'll likely receive thorough instructions on the proper use of equipment and safety measures. This ensures that participants can fully enjoy the experience with confidence and peace of mind.

For those seeking an escape from the ordinary, zip-lining at Cannonsburg Ski Area is an opportunity to step outside your comfort zone and embrace the thrill of adventure. Whether you're a seasoned zip-liner or a first-time participant, the experience promises a memorable journey through the treetops, creating lasting memories of your time in the scenic outdoors of Grand Rapids. Be sure to check with Cannonsburg Ski Area for specific details on zip-lining sessions, reservations, and any additional information to make the most of your adventure.

85.Attend the GRandJazzFest.

Embarking on a zip-lining adventure at Cannonsburg Ski Area in Grand Rapids promises an exhilarating experience surrounded by nature's beauty. Cannonsburg Ski Area, renowned for its winter sports offerings, transforms into an exciting destination for zip-lining during the warmer months. As you soar through the treetops, you'll be treated to panoramic views of the lush landscape, creating a perfect fusion of adrenaline-pumping action and natural splendor.

Cannonsburg Ski Area typically features a well-designed zip-lining course that caters to both thrill-seekers and nature enthusiasts. The zip lines are strategically positioned to provide an immersive experience, allowing participants to glide seamlessly through the trees and appreciate the scenic beauty of the Michigan outdoors.

Before embarking on your zip-lining adventure, you'll likely receive comprehensive safety instructions and be equipped with the necessary gear. This ensures that you can enjoy the exhilarating ride with confidence, knowing that safety measures are in place.

What sets zip-lining at Cannonsburg Ski Area apart is the harmonious blend of adventure and the serenity of nature. The zip lines are often integrated into the natural environment, offering a unique perspective of the surrounding landscape. Whether you're an experienced zip-liner or a first-timer, the thrill of zooming through the treetops creates an unforgettable and adrenaline-fueled experience.

For those seeking an escape into the great outdoors and an adrenaline rush, zip-lining at Cannonsburg Ski Area is a perfect choice. Before your adventure, it's advisable to check with the ski area for specific details on zip-lining sessions, reservations, and any other relevant information to ensure a seamless and enjoyable experience. Get ready to embrace the excitement and breathtaking views that await you at Cannonsburg Ski Area's zip-lining course in Grand Rapids.

86.Explore the Oakdale neighborhood.

Exploring the Oakdale neighborhood in Grand Rapids unveils a charming and diverse community with distinctive features and attractions. Oakdale is known for its residential character, local amenities, and community spirit. As you navigate through its streets, you'll encounter a variety of noteworthy aspects:

The Oakdale neighborhood is characterized by a mix of residential properties, ranging from historic homes to more modern constructions. The architecture reflects the neighborhood's evolution over time, providing a visual timeline of its development. Tree-lined streets and well-maintained properties contribute to the overall aesthetic appeal.

Local parks and green spaces are integral to the Oakdale community, offering residents and visitors places to relax, exercise, and enjoy outdoor activities. These green havens provide a sense of tranquility and foster a strong sense of community engagement.

Oakdale is likely to have a diverse range of local businesses, including small shops, cafes, and restaurants. Exploring these establishments provides an opportunity to support local entrepreneurs and experience the neighborhood's unique culinary and retail offerings.

Community events and gatherings may be a regular occurrence in Oakdale, fostering a strong sense of unity among residents. Whether it's neighborhood block parties, festivals, or farmers' markets, these events contribute to the vibrant social fabric of the community.

Local schools and educational institutions play a crucial role in Oakdale, providing resources for families and contributing to the neighborhood's family-friendly atmosphere. Educational facilities may include elementary schools, community centers, and libraries.

The Oakdale neighborhood is likely to have a diverse demographic, contributing to a rich cultural tapestry. Engaging with residents from various backgrounds provides an opportunity to learn about different perspectives and experiences, enhancing the sense of community belonging.

Access to essential services, such as healthcare facilities, places of worship, and public transportation, is an important aspect of Oakdale's infrastructure. Convenient access to these amenities enhances the overall livability of the neighborhood.

Cultural and recreational venues may be scattered throughout Oakdale, offering residents opportunities for entertainment and enrichment. This might include art galleries, performance spaces, or community theaters that add to the neighborhood's cultural vibrancy.

Before embarking on your exploration of the Oakdale neighborhood, it's advisable to check local community websites, events calendars, or neighborhood associations for any upcoming activities or points of interest. This ensures you can make the most of your visit and fully appreciate the unique charm and offerings that define Oakdale in Grand Rapids.

87.Go paddleboarding on Reeds Lake.

Embarking on a paddleboarding adventure on Reeds Lake in Grand Rapids promises a serene and picturesque experience surrounded by natural beauty. Reeds Lake, located in the East Grand Rapids area, is renowned for its clear waters and peaceful ambiance, making it an ideal spot for paddleboarding enthusiasts. As you glide along the surface of the lake, several aspects contribute to the allure of this activity:

Reeds Lake offers calm waters, providing an excellent environment for paddleboarding, whether you're a novice or an experienced paddler. The serene atmosphere creates a tranquil setting for a leisurely paddle or a more invigorating workout, depending on your preference.

The lake's scenic surroundings contribute to the overall charm of the paddleboarding experience. Reeds Lake is bordered by lush greenery and residential areas, providing a picturesque backdrop as you navigate its waters. The shoreline's beauty adds a delightful element to your paddleboarding excursion.

Paddleboarding on Reeds Lake allows you to connect with nature and enjoy the outdoors. The lake's ecosystem may include sightings of local wildlife, such as birds and fish, enhancing the immersive experience and providing moments of natural serenity.

The East Grand Rapids area, with its upscale residential character, contributes to the overall ambiance of Reeds Lake. Paddleboarding becomes not only a physical activity but also an opportunity to explore the neighborhood from a unique perspective, appreciating the lakeside residences and the community's well-maintained environment.

Before embarking on your paddleboarding adventure, ensure you have the necessary equipment, including a paddleboard and a personal flotation device. Additionally, familiarize yourself with any local regulations or guidelines related to paddleboarding on Reeds Lake.

Whether you choose to paddle at a leisurely pace, enjoy the lake's tranquility, or engage in a more active workout, paddleboarding on Reeds Lake provides a delightful escape into nature within the heart of Grand Rapids. Be sure to check weather conditions, and take in the sights and sounds as you navigate the calm waters of this scenic and beloved lake.

88. Attend the West Michigan Chalk Art Festival.

Attending the West Michigan Chalk Art Festival in Grand Rapids promises an immersive and visually stunning experience celebrating the vibrant world of chalk artistry. This annual festival typically transforms public spaces into colorful canvases where artists showcase their creativity in a variety of chalk-based masterpieces. Here are some highlights you can expect from your visit to the West Michigan Chalk Art Festival:

The festival serves as a dynamic platform for local and regional artists to showcase their talent, turning sidewalks and public spaces into temporary art galleries. You'll have the opportunity to witness the transformation of plain pavement into intricate, vivid artworks, each telling a unique story.

Artists participating in the Chalk Art Festival often come from diverse backgrounds, contributing to a rich tapestry of artistic styles and themes. From traditional to contemporary, the artwork on display reflects a wide range of inspirations, creating a visually captivating and eclectic atmosphere.

The festival typically encourages interactive engagement, allowing attendees to witness the creative process firsthand. You may have the chance to chat with artists, learn about their techniques, and gain insights into the stories behind their chalk creations.

In addition to professional artists, the West Michigan Chalk Art Festival often includes a "Community Chalk" component, where individuals of all ages can express their artistic flair. This collaborative effort adds a communal and inclusive dimension to the festival.

As you explore the festival grounds, live entertainment and music performances may accompany the visual spectacle, enhancing the overall festive atmosphere. The combination of vibrant artwork and lively performances creates a dynamic and enjoyable experience for attendees.

Photography opportunities abound, providing a chance to capture the ephemeral beauty of the chalk art before it eventually fades away. The festival encourages attendees to document and share their favorite creations, fostering a sense of community appreciation for the ephemeral nature of chalk art.

The West Michigan Chalk Art Festival typically draws a diverse crowd of art enthusiasts, families, and community members. This communal gathering fosters a positive and celebratory atmosphere, making it a perfect outing for individuals of all ages.

Before attending, it's advisable to check the festival's official website or local event listings for specific details regarding dates, participating artists, and any additional activities or special features. Whether you're a seasoned art aficionado or simply looking for a visually captivating experience, the West Michigan Chalk Art Festival offers a unique and vibrant celebration of artistic expression in the heart of Grand Rapids.

89.Explore the Ottawa Hills neighborhood.

Exploring the Ottawa Hills neighborhood in Grand Rapids unveils a picturesque and well-established community known for its tree-lined streets, historic homes, and family-friendly atmosphere. Here are some highlights you might discover during your visit to this charming neighborhood:

Historic Architecture: Ottawa Hills boasts an array of historic homes, showcasing a variety of architectural styles. The neighborhood's character is defined by the timeless elegance of these houses, providing a glimpse into its rich history.

Scenic Green Spaces: The neighborhood is dotted with parks and green spaces, offering residents and visitors serene spots to relax, play, and enjoy nature. These areas contribute to the overall sense of tranquility and provide opportunities for outdoor activities.

Community Schools: Ottawa Hills is home to reputable schools, contributing to its appeal for families. The neighborhood often fosters a strong sense of community around educational institutions, creating a supportive environment for residents with school-age children.

Family-Friendly Atmosphere: With its tree-lined streets, sidewalks, and parks, Ottawa Hills is known for its family-friendly ambiance. The neighborhood provides a safe and welcoming environment for families to thrive and create lasting memories.

Cultural Diversity: Ottawa Hills is often characterized by its diverse community, contributing to a rich cultural tapestry. Residents from various backgrounds create a harmonious blend of traditions and perspectives, adding to the neighborhood's vibrancy.

Local Businesses: Explore local businesses, shops, and cafes that contribute to the unique character of Ottawa Hills. These establishments often reflect the neighborhood's commitment to supporting local entrepreneurs and fostering a sense of community.

Historic Landmarks: Discover any historic landmarks or points of interest within Ottawa Hills. These landmarks may offer insights into the neighborhood's past and cultural heritage, providing a deeper understanding of its significance.

Community Events: Ottawa Hills may host community events and gatherings, such as block parties, festivals, or farmers' markets. Participating in these events allows you to connect with neighbors and experience the tight-knit community spirit.

Culinary Delights: Explore local dining options, whether it's a cozy cafe, family-friendly restaurant, or a hidden gem. Ottawa Hills may offer diverse culinary experiences, allowing you to savor flavors reflective of the community.

Community Engagement: Engage with local organizations, community groups, or neighborhood associations. These entities often play a vital role in organizing events, addressing local concerns, and enhancing the overall quality of life in Ottawa Hills.

Before your visit, consider checking community websites, local news sources, or neighborhood associations for any upcoming events or specific points of interest in Ottawa Hills. This ensures you can make the most of your exploration and fully appreciate the unique charm and community spirit that define this Grand Rapids neighborhood.

90.Go snowshoeing at Provin Trails Park.

Embarking on a snowshoeing adventure at Provin Trails Park in Grand Rapids promises a winter wonderland experience amidst the natural beauty of the park. Provin Trails, known for its scenic trails and lush landscapes, transforms into a serene and snowy landscape during the winter months. Here's what you can anticipate during your snowshoeing excursion:

Tranquil Winter Setting: Provin Trails Park, draped in a blanket of snow, offers a serene and tranquil setting. The crisp winter air and the pristine snow-covered trails create an idyllic atmosphere for a snowshoeing adventure.

Snow-Covered Trails: The park's well-maintained trails become a snowy playground for outdoor enthusiasts. Snowshoeing allows you to explore these trails at a leisurely pace, immersing yourself in the winter scenery while getting some invigorating exercise.

Connection with Nature: Snowshoeing at Provin Trails provides an opportunity to connect with nature in its winter splendor. The sound of snow crunching beneath your snowshoes, the sight of snow-laden branches, and the possibility of encountering winter wildlife contribute to a sensory-rich experience.

Accessible for All Skill Levels: Whether you're a seasoned snowshoer or a beginner, Provin Trails Park typically offers trails suitable for various skill levels. This inclusivity makes it an inviting destination for individuals or groups with different levels of snowshoeing expertise.

Winter Wildlife Sightings: Winter often brings unique opportunities for wildlife sightings. As you traverse the snow-covered trails, keep an eye out for tracks and signs of local wildlife. Provin Trails Park may offer a chance to observe winter-adapted animals in their natural habitat.

Exercise and Recreation: Snowshoeing provides an excellent cardiovascular workout and a chance to engage in recreational activities during the winter months. It's a low-impact exercise suitable for all ages, making it a family-friendly option for winter recreation.

Scenic Overlooks: If Provin Trails Park features elevated areas or scenic overlooks, snowshoeing allows you to reach these vantage points and enjoy panoramic views of the winter landscape. These viewpoints often reward snowshoers with stunning vistas of snow-covered terrain.

Winter Photography Opportunities: The snow-covered scenery at Provin Trails Park creates a picturesque backdrop, offering opportunities for winter photography. Capture the beauty of the landscape, the play of light on the snow, and the unique aspects of winter flora and fauna.

Before embarking on your snowshoeing adventure, ensure you have the appropriate snowshoe equipment, dress warmly, and check trail conditions. Provin Trails Park is likely to provide an enchanting winter escape for those seeking a peaceful and snowy outdoor experience in the heart of Grand Rapids.

91.Attend the International Wine, Beer & Food Festival.

Attending the International Wine, Beer & Food Festival in Grand Rapids promises a delectable and culturally enriching experience, showcasing the finest in global cuisine and beverages. This annual festival, held in the heart of the city, brings together a diverse array of culinary delights, craft beers, and exquisite wines. Here's what you can anticipate during your visit to this internationally inspired gastronomic event:

Global Culinary Delights: The festival is a culinary journey featuring a diverse range of international cuisines. From tantalizing appetizers to decadent desserts, attendees can savor flavors from around the world, highlighting the richness and diversity of global gastronomy.

Fine Wines: Wine enthusiasts will have the opportunity to explore an extensive selection of fine wines from various regions. Whether you prefer red, white, or sparkling varieties, the festival typically offers a curated collection of wines for tasting and appreciation.

Craft Beers and Brews: For beer connoisseurs, the International Wine, Beer & Food Festival showcases an impressive array of craft beers and brews. Attendees can sample a variety of styles, including unique and locally crafted options, providing a comprehensive beer-tasting experience.

Gastronomic Pairings: One of the highlights of the festival is the emphasis on pairing exquisite food with the perfect wine or beer. Expertly curated pairings enhance the tasting experience, allowing attendees to discover complementary flavors and textures.

Educational Workshops: The festival often includes educational workshops and seminars conducted by industry experts. These sessions may cover topics such as wine appreciation, brewing techniques, and culinary trends, providing attendees with valuable insights into the world of food and beverages.

Live Entertainment: Beyond the culinary delights, the festival typically features live entertainment to enhance the overall atmosphere. Whether it's live music, cultural performances, or interactive demonstrations, attendees can enjoy a vibrant and engaging experience.

Networking and Socializing: The International Wine, Beer & Food Festival provides an excellent opportunity for networking and socializing. Engage with fellow food and beverage enthusiasts, share recommendations, and connect with industry professionals in a convivial setting.

Artisan Exhibitors: Explore artisan exhibitors showcasing unique and handcrafted products related to the culinary world. From specialty foods to kitchen accessories, these exhibitors add an extra layer of exploration to the festival experience.

Culinary Competitions: Some festivals include culinary competitions where chefs showcase their skills in friendly contests. Witnessing these competitions adds an element of excitement and allows attendees to appreciate the artistry behind culinary creations.

Before attending, check the festival's official website for specific details on participating vendors, event schedules, and any additional attractions. The International Wine, Beer & Food Festival in Grand Rapids offers a delightful fusion of flavors, creating a memorable and immersive experience for those who appreciate the finer aspects of food and beverage culture.

92. Explore the Garfield Park neighborhood.

Exploring the Garfield Park neighborhood in Grand Rapids reveals a community with a rich history, diverse character, and a mix of residential and recreational offerings. Here's what you might discover during your visit to this dynamic neighborhood:

Historical Significance: Garfield Park has a history that contributes to the overall character of the neighborhood. Explore any historical landmarks or sites that showcase its past, offering insights into its development over the years.

Residential Diversity: The neighborhood is likely to feature a mix of housing styles, from historic homes to more modern residences. Take a stroll through the streets to appreciate the architectural diversity and the unique charm of Garfield Park's residential areas.

Community Parks: Garfield Park is known for its green spaces and community parks. These areas provide residents and visitors with places to relax, play, and engage in outdoor activities. Enjoy the natural surroundings and perhaps participate in recreational opportunities available in the parks.

Local Businesses: Explore local businesses, shops, and cafes that contribute to the neighborhood's commercial character. Garfield Park may have a variety of establishments, creating a vibrant and bustling atmosphere reflective of the community's commercial diversity.

Cultural and Community Events: Check for any cultural or community events taking place in Garfield Park. These events could include festivals, markets, or gatherings that bring residents together, fostering a sense of community spirit and engagement.

Schools and Educational Facilities: Garfield Park is likely to have educational institutions within its boundaries. Explore local schools, libraries, or community centers that play a role in the educational and cultural enrichment of the neighborhood.

Community Centers: Look for community centers or gathering spaces that serve as hubs for residents. These centers may host events, programs, and activities that contribute to the overall well-being and cohesion of the community.

Artistic Expressions: Garfield Park may feature artistic expressions such as murals, sculptures, or public art installations. These creative elements often add visual interest to the neighborhood and contribute to its cultural identity.

Local Parks and Recreation: Beyond community parks, Garfield Park may offer additional recreational facilities. These could include sports fields, walking trails, or other amenities that promote an active and healthy lifestyle.

Transportation Accessibility: Assess the accessibility of Garfield Park in terms of public transportation and roadways. Understanding the transportation options helps you navigate the neighborhood efficiently and connect with surrounding areas.

Before your visit, consider checking with local community sources, neighborhood associations, or event calendars for any upcoming activities or points of interest in Garfield Park. Exploring this neighborhood allows you to connect with its unique identity, appreciate its cultural richness, and experience the everyday life of residents in Grand Rapids.

93.Attend the Grand Rapids Film Festival.

Attending the Grand Rapids Film Festival offers a captivating cinematic experience, celebrating the art of filmmaking and providing a platform for diverse storytelling. Here's what you can anticipate during your visit to this dynamic film festival:

Film Screenings: The heart of the festival lies in its diverse selection of film screenings. Attendees have the opportunity to view a wide range of films, including feature-length movies, documentaries, short films, and possibly even experimental or independent productions. The curated lineup often reflects a variety of genres, themes, and storytelling styles.

Filmmaker Q&A Sessions: Many film festivals, including the Grand Rapids Film Festival, often feature Q&A sessions with filmmakers. This provides an invaluable opportunity to gain insights into the creative process, the inspiration behind the films, and the challenges faced during production.

Panel Discussions and Workshops: The festival may host panel discussions and workshops covering various aspects of the film industry. Topics could include filmmaking techniques, storytelling strategies, industry trends, and the intersection of film with social or cultural issues. Engaging with these discussions enhances the overall festival experience.

Cinematic Diversity: Film festivals are known for showcasing a diverse range of voices and perspectives. The Grand Rapids Film Festival likely emphasizes inclusivity, presenting films that explore different cultures, backgrounds, and viewpoints. This diversity contributes to a rich and enlightening cinematic experience.

Networking Opportunities: Attendees, including filmmakers, actors, and film enthusiasts, often gather at the festival. Networking events may provide opportunities to connect with professionals in the film industry, exchange ideas, and build relationships within the filmmaking community.

Celebrity Appearances: Depending on the festival's scale and prominence, there might be appearances by filmmakers, actors, or industry figures. These encounters can add an exciting element to the festival experience, allowing fans and aspiring filmmakers to connect with established professionals.

Awards and Recognitions: Film festivals frequently conclude with awards ceremonies, acknowledging outstanding achievements in various categories.

Attendees can witness the recognition of exceptional filmmaking talent and celebrate the contributions of filmmakers to the cinematic landscape.

Film Market and Exhibitions: Some festivals incorporate film markets or exhibitions where industry professionals showcase their work, explore potential collaborations, and discuss distribution opportunities. This aspect adds a business-oriented dimension to the festival, fostering connections within the film industry.

Cinematic Atmosphere: The festival atmosphere is often vibrant and cinematic, with venues adorned in film-related decor. The energy and excitement among attendees create a unique environment, emphasizing the communal appreciation of film as an art form.

Before attending, check the Grand Rapids Film Festival's official website or event announcements for specific details regarding film schedules, guest appearances, and any additional activities. The festival promises an immersive cinematic experience, allowing you to discover new stories, engage with the filmmaking community, and celebrate the art of cinema in the heart of Grand Rapids.

94. Go cross-country skiing at Pigeon Creek Park.

Embarking on a cross-country skiing adventure at Pigeon Creek Park near Grand Rapids promises a winter wonderland experience surrounded by the natural beauty of the park. Here's what you can anticipate during your cross-country skiing excursion:

Tranquil Winter Setting: Pigeon Creek Park, covered in a blanket of snow, offers a serene and picturesque setting for cross-country skiing. The snow-laden trees, frozen landscapes, and the crisp winter air create a tranquil atmosphere, making it an ideal location for winter sports.

Well-Maintained Trails: Pigeon Creek Park is known for its well-maintained trails that cater to cross-country skiers of various skill levels. The park typically offers a network of groomed trails, allowing skiers to explore the winter landscape in a controlled and enjoyable manner.

Scenic Wooded Areas: The park's trails often wind through scenic wooded areas, providing skiers with an immersive experience in nature. The snow-covered trees and the hushed ambiance of the winter forest add to the beauty of the cross-country skiing journey.

Trail Variety: Pigeon Creek Park may feature a variety of trails, including loops of different lengths and difficulty levels. Whether you're a beginner or an experienced skier, you can choose a trail that suits your skill and fitness level, creating a personalized and enjoyable experience.

Winter Wildlife Sightings: While cross-country skiing, keep an eye out for winter wildlife. Pigeon Creek Park's natural environment may offer glimpses of animals adapted to the winter season, adding a touch of wildlife observation to your skiing adventure.

Family-Friendly Atmosphere: Cross-country skiing at Pigeon Creek Park is often family-friendly, providing an opportunity for individuals of all ages to enjoy the winter sport together. The park's inclusive environment makes it an ideal destination for a winter outing with family and friends.

Winter Recreation Hub: Pigeon Creek Park is a popular hub for winter recreation, and cross-country skiing is just one of the activities available. The park may also offer amenities such as snowshoeing, sledding, and winter hiking, providing a range of options for outdoor enthusiasts.

Winter Photography Opportunities: The picturesque winter scenery at Pigeon Creek Park provides ample opportunities for capturing memorable moments through photography. Consider bringing a camera to document the beauty of the snow-covered landscape and your cross-country skiing adventure.

Before heading out, ensure you have the appropriate cross-country skiing equipment, dress warmly, and check trail conditions. Pigeon Creek Park's commitment to winter sports and its scenic trails make it an inviting destination for those seeking an active and visually stunning winter experience in the Grand Rapids area.

95. Attend a beer or wine tasting event.

Attending a beer or wine tasting event in Grand Rapids promises a delightful experience, given the city's reputation for its craft beer scene and burgeoning wine culture. Here's what you can expect and explore during such an event:

Craft Beer Tasting:

Local Breweries: Grand Rapids is known for its vibrant craft beer scene. Attend a beer tasting event hosted by one of the city's many local breweries. Popular ones include Founders Brewing Co., Brewery Vivant, and The Mitten Brewing Company.
Variety of Brews: Expect a diverse selection of craft beers, from hoppy IPAs to rich stouts and everything in between. Tasting flights are often offered, allowing you to sample a variety of brews in smaller quantities.
Wine Tasting:

Local Wineries: While Grand Rapids is more famous for its beer, there are also wineries in the surrounding region. Explore a wine tasting event featuring local wines. Check out nearby wineries like Fenn Valley Vineyards or Cascade Winery for tastings.
Wine Varietals: Experience a range of wine varietals, from crisp whites to bold reds. Learn about the characteristics of different wines and perhaps discover new favorites.
Pairing Events:

Food Pairings: Some tasting events include food pairings to complement the beverages. Local chefs often collaborate with breweries or wineries to create a culinary experience that enhances the flavors of the drinks.
Educational Sessions: Attendees may have the opportunity to participate in educational sessions, where experts discuss the art of pairing beer or wine with food. This can add a layer of sophistication to the tasting experience.
Live Entertainment:

Music and Atmosphere: Tasting events often feature live music or a vibrant atmosphere. Enjoy the tunes while sipping on your favorite beverages, creating a social and enjoyable ambiance.
Meet Brewers or Vintners:

Meet the Makers: Some events provide the chance to meet the brewers or vintners behind the beverages. This personal touch allows you to learn more about the craft and passion that goes into creating each drink.
Local Festivals or Events:

Beer or Wine Festivals: Grand Rapids hosts various beer and wine festivals throughout the year. These larger-scale events gather a wide array of local and regional breweries or wineries, offering a comprehensive tasting experience. Ticketed Events:

Purchase Tickets: Many beer or wine tastings require tickets, which can often be purchased in advance. Check event websites or local listings to secure your spot at the tasting of your choice.

96.Attend the Local First Street Party.

Attending the Local First Street Party in Grand Rapids promises a vibrant celebration of community, local businesses, and the unique culture that defines the city. Here's what you can anticipate during your visit to this lively event:

Community Celebration:

The Local First Street Party is a community-driven event that celebrates the spirit and resilience of Grand Rapids. It often brings together residents, local businesses, and visitors for a day of festivities.
Local Businesses Showcase:

The street party typically features a showcase of local businesses, artisans, and vendors. Explore booths and displays to discover unique products, handmade crafts, and services offered by entrepreneurs in the Grand Rapids area.
Live Music and Entertainment:

Enjoy the lively atmosphere with live music performances by local bands and artists. The street party often hosts a diverse range of musical genres, providing a soundtrack to the festivities.
Food and Beverage Options:

Indulge in a variety of culinary delights from local food trucks and vendors. Taste the flavors of Grand Rapids with a selection of delicious dishes, snacks, and beverages.
Family-Friendly Activities:

The event is usually family-friendly, offering activities for children and adults alike. Expect face painting, interactive games, and other entertainment suitable for families.
Art and Culture:

Immerse yourself in the local art scene with displays of visual arts, performances, and cultural exhibits. The Local First Street Party often highlights the creativity and talent within the Grand Rapids community.
Sustainability and Local Initiatives:

Local First often emphasizes sustainability and community initiatives. Learn about eco-friendly practices, local sustainability projects, and how the community is working together to create a positive impact.
Networking Opportunities:

The street party provides a great opportunity for networking and socializing. Connect with fellow community members, local business owners, and like-minded individuals who share a passion for supporting the local economy.
Educational Workshops and Talks:

Engage in educational workshops or talks that focus on topics such as sustainable living, local business success stories, or community development. These sessions can provide valuable insights and inspiration.
Street Performers and Art Installations:

Be on the lookout for street performers and interactive art installations that add an element of surprise and creativity to the event. These elements contribute to the unique and dynamic atmosphere of the Local First Street Party.
Before attending, check the event's official website or local listings for specific details, such as the schedule, participating businesses, and any additional attractions. The Local First Street Party offers a wonderful opportunity to immerse yourself in the vibrant and supportive community spirit of Grand Rapids.

97.Go geocaching in local parks.

Embarking on a geocaching adventure in local parks around Grand Rapids offers an exciting and interactive way to explore the outdoors while engaging in a treasure hunt. Here's what you can anticipate during your geocaching experience:

Geocaching Basics:

Geocaching involves using GPS coordinates to locate hidden containers, or "caches," placed by other participants. These caches can be found in various locations, including parks, urban areas, and natural settings.
Selecting Parks:

Grand Rapids and its surrounding areas likely have numerous parks with geocaching opportunities. Choose parks that align with your preferences, whether you prefer wooded areas, scenic landscapes, or urban settings.
GPS Device or Smartphone App:

Ensure you have a GPS device or a geocaching app on your smartphone. Popular apps include Geocaching by Groundspeak or Cachly. These apps provide information about nearby caches, navigation tools, and user logs.
Cache Variety:

Geocaches come in various sizes and difficulty levels. Some may be small containers with only a logbook, while others may include trinkets for trading. Check the cache details before heading out to understand what to expect.
Scenic Trails and Nature Walks:

Many geocaches are hidden along scenic trails and nature walks. Use this opportunity to explore the natural beauty of local parks. Trails in places like Millennium Park or Blandford Nature Center might offer geocaching options.
Family-Friendly Adventure:

Geocaching is a family-friendly activity. Choose parks with easier caches if you're geocaching with children. It's a fantastic way to involve the whole family in an outdoor adventure.
Respecting Nature and Park Rules:

While geocaching, be mindful of the environment and follow park rules. Stay on designated trails, respect wildlife, and adhere to any specific guidelines set by the park authorities.
Community and Events:

Check for local geocaching events or communities in the Grand Rapids area. Participating in events can enhance your geocaching experience and connect you with other enthusiasts.
Logbook Signings:

Each geocache has a logbook where finders can sign their geocaching usernames and the date of discovery. Share your experiences in the logbook and read entries from previous finders.
BYOP (Bring Your Own Pencil):

Some smaller caches may not have writing instruments. Be prepared by bringing your own pencil or pen to sign logbooks.
Before starting your geocaching adventure, familiarize yourself with the rules and etiquette of geocaching, respect private property, and prioritize safety. Check online platforms or apps for the latest information on available caches, and enjoy the thrill of discovering hidden treasures in the parks around Grand Rapids.

98.Attend the GR Hiking & Yoga Meetup events.

Participating in the GR Hiking & Yoga Meetup events in Grand Rapids promises a harmonious blend of outdoor activities, fitness, and community engagement. Here's what you can expect when attending these events:

Hiking Adventures:

Explore the scenic trails around Grand Rapids as part of the hiking events. The group may visit various parks and natural areas, offering a chance to discover the beauty of the local landscape.
Fitness and Wellness:

The combination of hiking and yoga provides a holistic approach to fitness and wellness. Hiking engages your cardiovascular system and muscles, while yoga offers stretching, balance, and mindfulness, promoting overall well-being.
Community Connection:

Meet like-minded individuals who share an interest in both hiking and yoga. These events provide a social and supportive environment, fostering connections with people who value outdoor activities and healthy lifestyles.
Variety of Locations:

Travel to Grand Rapids Michigan

The group may explore different hiking trails and yoga venues across Grand Rapids. This variety adds excitement to each event and allows participants to experience diverse natural settings.

All Skill Levels Welcome:

Whether you're an experienced hiker and yogi or a beginner, these meetups are often designed to accommodate all skill levels. Joining the events is a great way to learn from others and enhance your skills in both activities.

Mindful Outdoor Experience:

Engage in mindfulness practices during both hiking and yoga sessions. Enjoy the tranquility of nature, breathe in the fresh air, and appreciate the present moment as you connect with the outdoors.

Organized Meetup Structure:

The GR Hiking & Yoga Meetup events are likely organized with a structured schedule. This could include a group hike, a yoga session at a scenic location, and perhaps a time for socializing or sharing experiences.

Health and Fitness Goals:

For those aiming to maintain an active and healthy lifestyle, these events contribute to achieving fitness goals. The combination of cardiovascular exercise, strength-building through hiking, and flexibility from yoga aligns with a holistic approach to health.

Positive and Inclusive Atmosphere:

Meetup groups often prioritize creating a positive and inclusive atmosphere. Whether you come alone or with friends, you're likely to feel welcomed by a community of individuals who appreciate the benefits of outdoor activities.

Event Updates and Information:

Stay informed about upcoming events by regularly checking the Meetup group's page or communication channels. This ensures you have the latest details on locations, times, and any additional information for each event.

Before attending, consider checking the Meetup group's guidelines, any equipment or attire recommendations, and if there are any costs associated with specific events. Embrace the opportunity to enjoy the outdoors, meet new people, and enhance your well-being through the GR Hiking & Yoga Meetup events in Grand Rapids.

99.Explore the Cheshire Village neighborhood.

Cheshire Village is primarily a residential neighborhood, characterized by tree-lined streets and a mix of housing styles. It often attracts residents seeking a balance between a suburban atmosphere and proximity to urban amenities.
Local Businesses:

Explore local businesses and shops in Cheshire Village. You might find quaint boutiques, coffee shops, and other establishments that contribute to the neighborhood's charm.
Cheshire Business District:

The Cheshire Business District is known for its small businesses and community-focused establishments. It's a hub where locals gather for shopping, dining, and socializing.
Cheshire Grill:

The Cheshire Grill is a popular spot in the neighborhood, known for its classic diner-style atmosphere and comfort food. It's a local favorite for breakfast and lunch.
Community Events:

Cheshire Village may host community events throughout the year, such as neighborhood gatherings, markets, or festivals. These events contribute to the sense of community in the area.
Neighborhood Parks:

Check out any nearby parks or green spaces. Parks provide opportunities for outdoor activities, picnics, and a place for residents to enjoy nature.
Local Schools:

If you have an interest in educational institutions, explore local schools in the Cheshire Village area. Schools often play a central role in fostering a sense of community.
Architectural Diversity:

Cheshire Village likely features a mix of architectural styles in its homes, showcasing the diversity of the neighborhood. This can add character and visual interest to the area.
Walkable Streets:

Enjoy a stroll through the neighborhood's walkable streets. Cheshire Village is designed to be pedestrian-friendly, allowing residents and visitors to explore on foot.
Community Engagement:

Cheshire Village may have an active neighborhood association or community groups. Engage with these organizations to stay informed about local happenings and connect with your neighbors.
Remember that neighborhoods can evolve, and new developments or changes may occur. For the latest and most accurate information about Cheshire Village, consider checking with local community centers, city planning departments, or residents' associations for updates and insights.

100.Go disc golfing at Johnson Park.

Disc golfing at Johnson Park in Grand Rapids promises an enjoyable outdoor experience surrounded by nature. Here's what you can anticipate during your disc golf adventure at Johnson Park:

Scenic Setting:

Johnson Park is known for its scenic beauty, offering a picturesque backdrop for a round of disc golf. The course is likely set amidst trees, meadows, and natural landscapes, providing a tranquil environment for players.
Disc Golf Course Layout:

Explore the layout of the disc golf course at Johnson Park. Courses typically consist of a series of holes with designated tee-off areas and target baskets. The layout may take you through various terrains, adding variety to your game.
Challenging Holes:

Expect a mix of hole difficulties. Disc golf courses often incorporate a range of challenges, including wooded areas, open fields, and elevation changes. Each hole presents a unique set of obstacles that require skill and strategy to navigate.
Equipment and Rules:

Bring your own disc golf set or rent one if available. Familiarize yourself with the rules of disc golf, including the number of throws allowed per hole and any specific course rules implemented at Johnson Park.
Community Atmosphere:

Disc golf is often a social and community-oriented activity. You may encounter other players enjoying the course. It's common for disc golfers to be friendly and welcoming, making it an inclusive sport for all skill levels.
Nature Walk and Exercise:

Disc golfing at Johnson Park combines the enjoyment of the game with the benefits of outdoor exercise. Walking the course allows you to appreciate nature and stay active during your rounds.
Family-Friendly Activity:

Disc golf is a family-friendly activity suitable for all ages. If you're with family or friends, it provides an opportunity for shared enjoyment in an outdoor setting.
Park Amenities:

Johnson Park may have additional amenities for visitors. Explore the park's facilities, such as picnic areas, walking trails, or recreational spaces, to extend your outdoor experience beyond disc golf.
Events and Tournaments:

Check if there are any disc golf events or tournaments happening at Johnson Park. Participating in organized events can add a competitive and community aspect to your disc golfing experience.
Respect for the Environment:

Practice Leave No Trace principles and respect the natural environment. Disc golf courses are typically situated in public parks, and preserving the beauty of the surroundings is crucial for the enjoyment of all visitors.
Before heading to Johnson Park, check for any specific regulations, course maps, or updates on the park's website or local disc golfing community resources. Enjoy your disc golfing adventure in the scenic surroundings of Johnson Park!

101.Attend the Downtown Market Grand Rapids events.

Attending events at the Downtown Market in Grand Rapids offers a diverse and vibrant experience, combining culinary delights, local artisanal products, and community engagement. Here's what you can expect during your visit to the Downtown Market:

Local Food Vendors:

Explore a variety of local food vendors offering delicious and diverse cuisines. From gourmet restaurants to casual eateries, the Downtown Market is a culinary hub where you can savor a range of flavors.
Farmers Market:

If your visit coincides with a farmers market event, you'll have the opportunity to browse fresh, locally sourced produce, artisanal goods, and handmade products. Farmers markets at the Downtown Market showcase the region's agricultural offerings.
Cooking Classes and Demonstrations:

The Downtown Market often hosts cooking classes and culinary demonstrations. Join a class to enhance your cooking skills, learn from local chefs, and discover new recipes using fresh, local ingredients.
Artisanal Products:

Explore stalls and shops featuring artisanal products, including handmade crafts, specialty foods, and unique gifts. The market supports local artisans, providing a platform for them to showcase their talents.
Food and Beverage Events:

Keep an eye out for special food and beverage events. The Downtown Market may host tastings, pairing sessions, or themed events that celebrate the culinary diversity of Grand Rapids.
Community Gatherings:

The market serves as a gathering place for the community. Attend events that foster a sense of togetherness, such as outdoor concerts, festivals, or community celebrations.
Seasonal Offerings:

Events at the Downtown Market often reflect the changing seasons. Seasonal themes may influence the types of products, dishes, and activities available, providing a dynamic and evolving experience.
Educational Workshops:

Engage in educational workshops that focus on various aspects of food, nutrition, and sustainability. The market's events may include discussions and activities that promote awareness of local and sustainable practices.
Live Entertainment:

Enjoy live music, performances, or entertainment that enhances the overall atmosphere of the Downtown Market. Events may feature local artists and musicians, contributing to a lively and festive ambiance.
Outdoor Spaces:

Take advantage of outdoor spaces within the market. Outdoor seating areas provide a pleasant environment to enjoy your food, socialize, and soak in the atmosphere of the bustling market.
Before planning your visit, check the Downtown Market's official website or event calendar for the latest information on upcoming events, schedules, and any special features. Whether you're a food enthusiast, art lover, or simply looking for a vibrant community experience, the Downtown Market in Grand Rapids offers a dynamic and enjoyable destination.

102.Explore the Beckwith Hills neighborhood.

Beckwith Hills is primarily a residential area with a mix of single-family homes. The neighborhood often exhibits a suburban character, providing a quiet and family-friendly environment.
Tree-Lined Streets:

Expect tree-lined streets that contribute to a visually appealing and shaded atmosphere. The neighborhood's greenery and landscaping enhance the overall aesthetics.
Community Parks:

Explore any local parks or green spaces within or near Beckwith Hills. Parks offer opportunities for outdoor activities, picnics, and a place for residents to enjoy nature.
Schools and Education:

Beckwith Hills may have nearby schools, contributing to the sense of community and making it an attractive area for families with school-aged children.
Local Businesses:

While primarily residential, Beckwith Hills might have local businesses, convenience stores, or small shops that cater to the needs of residents.
Community Involvement:

Check if Beckwith Hills has an active neighborhood association or community groups. These organizations often play a role in organizing events, fostering a sense of community, and addressing local concerns.
Proximity to Amenities:

Assess the neighborhood's proximity to amenities such as shopping centers, healthcare facilities, and dining options. Beckwith Hills residents may have convenient access to essential services.
Transportation Access:

Consider the accessibility of transportation options. Beckwith Hills' location in relation to major roads and highways can impact commuting and connectivity to other parts of Grand Rapids.
Architectural Diversity:

Explore the architectural diversity of homes in Beckwith Hills. The neighborhood may feature a range of housing styles, contributing to a varied and interesting streetscape.
Quiet and Family-Friendly Atmosphere:

Beckwith Hills is often characterized by a peaceful and family-friendly atmosphere. Residents may appreciate the tranquility and sense of community that comes with living in a residential neighborhood.
To gather the latest and most accurate information about the Beckwith Hills neighborhood, consider reaching out to local real estate agents, community centers, or the city's planning department. Additionally, residents' reviews and online community forums can provide valuable insights into the current character and offerings of the neighborhood.

103.Go fishing at Reed's Lake in East Grand Rapids.

Fishing at Reed's Lake in East Grand Rapids offers a tranquil and picturesque setting for anglers to enjoy. Here's what you can expect during your fishing experience at Reed's Lake:

Scenic Setting:

Reed's Lake is known for its scenic beauty, surrounded by lush greenery and residential areas. The peaceful atmosphere creates a serene backdrop for a day of fishing.
Diverse Fish Species:

The lake is home to various fish species, and anglers may have the opportunity to catch a range of freshwater fish. Common species found in Reed's Lake include bass, bluegill, perch, and more.
Fishing from Shore:

If you prefer shore fishing, Reed's Lake provides accessible areas along its shoreline for anglers to set up and cast their lines. Find a comfortable spot and enjoy the view while waiting for the fish to bite.
Boat Fishing:

For those with access to a boat, Reed's Lake is navigable, allowing for boat fishing. Launch facilities are available, providing the opportunity to explore different areas of the lake for optimal fishing conditions.
Fishing Events and Tournaments:

Check for any fishing events or tournaments held at Reed's Lake. These occasions can add a competitive and community aspect to your fishing experience.
Fishing Regulations:

Familiarize yourself with fishing regulations and guidelines for Reed's Lake. Regulations may include catch limits, size restrictions, and specific rules designed to preserve the lake's ecosystem.
Peaceful Surroundings:

Reed's Lake offers a peaceful and calm environment. Whether you're fishing alone, with friends, or as a family, it's an opportunity to connect with nature and enjoy a quiet day by the water.
Local Fishing Tips:

Connect with local anglers or visit nearby bait and tackle shops for tips on the best fishing spots, preferred bait, and techniques for success at Reed's Lake.
Seasonal Considerations:

Be aware of seasonal variations in fish behavior. Different seasons may yield different fishing experiences, so plan your visit accordingly.
Picnic and Relaxation:

Take advantage of the lakeside setting by packing a picnic. Enjoy the scenery, take breaks between casts, and make the most of the relaxing ambiance that Reed's Lake provides.
Before heading out, it's advisable to check for any updates on fishing conditions, permits, and local regulations. Whether you're an experienced angler or a beginner, Reed's Lake offers a serene and enjoyable fishing experience in the heart of East Grand Rapids.

104. Attend a cooking class at the Downtown Market Grand Rapids.

Participating in a cooking class at the Downtown Market in Grand Rapids is a delightful and educational experience. Here's what you can look forward to during your cooking class:

Culinary Expertise:

Cooking classes at the Downtown Market are typically led by experienced chefs or culinary experts. These professionals bring their expertise and passion for food to the class, creating an enriching learning environment.
Variety of Classes:

The Downtown Market often offers a variety of cooking classes covering different cuisines, techniques, and skill levels. Whether you're a beginner or an experienced home cook, there's likely a class tailored to your interests.
Hands-On Experience:

Expect a hands-on cooking experience. Participants are usually provided with the opportunity to actively engage in preparing dishes, allowing for practical learning and skill development.
Local and Seasonal Ingredients:

Many cooking classes at the Downtown Market focus on using local and seasonal ingredients. This not only supports local producers but also emphasizes the importance of fresh, high-quality components in cooking.
Small Class Sizes:

Classes often have small group sizes, fostering a personalized and interactive setting. This allows participants to receive individualized attention and guidance from the instructor.
Recipe Demos:

In addition to hands-on cooking, instructors may demonstrate key techniques and share cooking tips. This combination of practical experience and visual demonstration enhances the learning process.
Tasting and Sharing:

Enjoy the fruits of your labor by tasting the dishes you've prepared during the class. It's also an opportunity to share your creations with fellow participants, fostering a sense of community and camaraderie.
Take-Home Recipes:

Participants typically receive printed or digital copies of the recipes used in the class. This allows you to recreate the dishes at home and continue practicing the skills you've learned.
Culinary Q&A:

Take advantage of the expertise of the instructor by asking questions about culinary techniques, ingredient choices, and any cooking-related inquiries you may have.
Networking and Socializing:

Cooking classes provide a social environment where you can connect with other food enthusiasts. It's a great opportunity to meet new people who share a common interest in cooking.
Before attending a cooking class, check the Downtown Market's schedule, class offerings, and registration details. Some classes may have specific themes, such as baking, ethnic cuisines, or special occasions. Whether you're a novice in the

kitchen or looking to refine your culinary skills, a cooking class at the
Downtown Market is sure to be a rewarding and enjoyable experience.

105.Explore the Mulick Park neighborhood.

Mulick Park is primarily a residential area, featuring a mix of single-family
homes. The neighborhood is often characterized by a suburban atmosphere,
providing a quiet and family-friendly environment.
Mulick Park:

The neighborhood is likely named after Mulick Park, which could be a central
green space offering recreational opportunities. Parks often serve as gathering
places for residents and provide areas for outdoor activities.
Schools and Education:

Explore local educational institutions in and around Mulick Park. Proximity to
schools is often a key factor for families, contributing to a sense of community
and making the area appealing for those with school-aged children.
Community Engagement:

Check if Mulick Park has an active neighborhood association or community
groups. These organizations may play a role in organizing events, addressing
local concerns, and fostering a sense of community among residents.
Proximity to Amenities:

Assess the neighborhood's accessibility to amenities such as shopping centers,
healthcare facilities, and dining options. Convenient access to essential services
enhances the overall appeal of Mulick Park.
Transportation Access:

Consider the accessibility of transportation options. Mulick Park's location in
relation to major roads and highways can impact commuting and connectivity to
other parts of Grand Rapids.
Recreational Opportunities:

Beyond parks, explore other recreational opportunities in Mulick Park. This
might include local sports facilities, walking trails, or community centers where
residents can engage in various activities.
Cultural Diversity:

Investigate the cultural diversity of Mulick Park. Neighborhoods often reflect a blend of cultures, contributing to a rich tapestry of community life.
Local Businesses:

While predominantly residential, Mulick Park may have local businesses, convenience stores, or small shops that cater to the needs of residents.
Architectural Diversity:

Explore the architectural diversity of homes in Mulick Park. Residential areas often feature a mix of housing styles, adding character and visual interest to the neighborhood.
To gather the latest and most accurate information about the Mulick Park neighborhood, consider reaching out to local real estate agents, community centers, or the city's planning department. Additionally, residents' reviews and online community forums can provide valuable insights into the current character and offerings of the neighborhood.

106.Go tubing or sledding at Cannonsburg Ski Area.

Tubing or sledding at Cannonsburg Ski Area in Grand Rapids promises a thrilling and enjoyable winter experience. Here's what you can expect during your tubing or sledding adventure at Cannonsburg:

Dedicated Tubing Lanes:

Cannonsburg Ski Area typically features dedicated tubing lanes designed for a safe and exhilarating experience. These lanes are groomed and maintained to provide optimal conditions for tubing.
Tube Rental Services:

If you don't have your own tube, Cannonsburg Ski Area usually offers tube rental services. This allows visitors to enjoy tubing without the need to bring their equipment.
Varied Terrain:

The ski area likely provides a variety of tubing lanes with different levels of difficulty. Whether you're seeking a gentle ride or a more adventurous descent, you'll find options suitable for various preferences.

Travel to Grand Rapids Michigan

Spectacular Views:

Enjoy scenic views of the winter landscape as you make your way down the tubing lanes. Cannonsburg Ski Area's location often provides picturesque surroundings, adding to the overall experience.
Family-Friendly Environment:

Tubing is a family-friendly activity, and Cannonsburg Ski Area is likely designed to accommodate visitors of all ages. It's a great way for families, friends, and individuals to enjoy the winter weather together.
Safety Measures:

Cannonsburg Ski Area prioritizes safety, and tubing facilities typically implement safety measures such as well-maintained lanes, designated tubing areas, and staff assistance as needed.
Snowmaking Capability:

In order to ensure a consistent and enjoyable tubing experience, Cannonsburg Ski Area may have snowmaking capabilities. This allows them to maintain suitable snow conditions throughout the winter season.
Après-Tubing Amenities:

After tubing, you might find amenities such as warming huts or a lodge where you can relax, warm up, and enjoy hot beverages. These spaces often contribute to the overall enjoyment of the winter outing.
Group Outings and Events:

Cannonsburg Ski Area may host group outings or special tubing events. Check their schedule for any themed tubing nights or events that add extra excitement to your visit.
Accessibility and Parking:

The ski area typically provides accessible parking and facilities. Plan your visit by checking their website or contacting them for information on parking, accessibility, and any specific guidelines.

107. Attend the Gerald R. Ford Memorial Day Parade.

Attending the Gerald R. Ford Memorial Day Parade in Grand Rapids is a patriotic and community-oriented experience, paying tribute to the legacy of President Gerald R. Ford and honoring those who have served in the military. Here's what you can expect during this Memorial Day parade:

Historical Significance:

The Gerald R. Ford Memorial Day Parade is likely to hold historical significance, commemorating the life and contributions of the 38th President of the United States, Gerald R. Ford, who served from 1974 to 1977.
Patriotic Atmosphere:

The parade is infused with a patriotic atmosphere, featuring displays of American flags, military tributes, and symbols of national pride. It serves as a way for the community to come together in remembrance.
Military Participation:

The parade often includes active-duty military personnel, veterans, and military vehicles. It provides an opportunity for the community to express gratitude and support for the men and women who have served or are currently serving in the armed forces.
Floats and Marching Bands:

Expect a procession of floats, marching bands, and community organizations. These participants may showcase patriotic themes, historical elements, and creative displays that add vibrancy to the parade.
Community Involvement:

The Memorial Day Parade is a community event, and local organizations, schools, and businesses may participate. It's a chance for residents to come together to celebrate shared values and express appreciation for the sacrifices made by military personnel.
Veterans Recognition:

Veterans are often prominently recognized during the parade. Special tributes, acknowledgments, and activities may be dedicated to honoring the service and dedication of veterans from various branches of the military.
Family-Friendly Atmosphere:

The parade is typically family-friendly, making it suitable for all ages. Families often attend together to instill a sense of patriotism and remembrance in younger generations.
Civic Pride:

The parade fosters a sense of civic pride and unity, reinforcing the importance of remembering and honoring those who have given their lives in service to the country.
Memorial Day Observance:

The parade is aligned with Memorial Day observances, emphasizing the solemnity and respect associated with the holiday. It serves as a meaningful way for the community to come together in reflection.
Local Tradition:

The Gerald R. Ford Memorial Day Parade may be a longstanding local tradition, attracting residents and visitors alike. It provides an opportunity for the community to express its values and commemorate the nation's history.
Before attending, check the event's official website or local community calendars for specific details, parade route information, and any related activities or ceremonies that may accompany the Memorial Day Parade in honor of Gerald R. Ford and those who have served in the military.

108.Explore the Shawmut Hills neighborhood.

Shawmut Hills is primarily a residential area, featuring a mix of single-family homes. The neighborhood is likely known for its suburban feel, providing a quiet and family-friendly environment.
Schools and Education:

Explore local educational institutions within or near Shawmut Hills. Proximity to schools often makes the neighborhood appealing to families with school-aged children.
Parks and Green Spaces:

Check for local parks or green spaces where residents can enjoy outdoor activities and recreation. Parks contribute to the quality of life in residential neighborhoods.

Community Involvement:

Look into the presence of a neighborhood association or community groups in Shawmut Hills. These organizations often play a role in organizing events, addressing local concerns, and fostering a sense of community.
Local Businesses:

While primarily residential, Shawmut Hills may have local businesses, convenience stores, or small shops that cater to the needs of residents.
Cultural and Recreational Facilities:

Explore any cultural or recreational facilities in or near the neighborhood. This could include community centers, sports facilities, or spaces for cultural events and gatherings.
Architectural Diversity:

Residential areas often feature a mix of architectural styles. Explore the diversity of home designs within Shawmut Hills, contributing to the overall character of the neighborhood.
Transportation Access:

Consider the accessibility of transportation options. Shawmut Hills' location in relation to major roads and highways can impact commuting and connectivity to other parts of Grand Rapids.
Local Events and Festivals:

Check for any local events or festivals that may take place in or around Shawmut Hills. These events contribute to the community spirit and provide opportunities for residents to come together.
Community Amenities:

Assess the availability of community amenities such as playgrounds, community centers, or gathering spaces. These amenities enhance the overall livability of a neighborhood.
To gather the latest and most accurate information about the Shawmut Hills neighborhood, consider reaching out to local real estate agents, community centers, or the city's planning department. Additionally, residents' reviews and online community forums can provide valuable insights into the current character and offerings of the neighborhood.

109.Go camping at PJ Hoffmaster State Park.

Camping at PJ Hoffmaster State Park near Grand Rapids promises a serene and nature-filled experience. Here's what you can expect during your camping adventure at PJ Hoffmaster State Park:

Campsites:

PJ Hoffmaster State Park likely offers a range of campsites to accommodate different preferences. This may include options for tents, RVs, and trailers, each providing a unique camping experience.
Natural Surroundings:

The park is known for its natural beauty, featuring wooded areas, sand dunes, and proximity to Lake Michigan. Expect stunning views and the opportunity to immerse yourself in the serene surroundings of the Michigan landscape.
Hiking Trails:

Explore hiking trails within the park. These trails may lead you through diverse ecosystems, offering a chance to observe local flora and fauna while enjoying the fresh air.
Beach Access:

PJ Hoffmaster State Park likely provides access to Lake Michigan's shoreline. Spend time on the beach, relax by the water, and perhaps take a refreshing swim during the warmer months.
Dune Climb:

Check if the park features a dune climb. Climbing the sand dunes provides a unique and invigorating experience, offering panoramic views of the surrounding landscape.
Visitor Center:

Visit the park's visitor center to learn more about the local ecology, wildlife, and the history of PJ Hoffmaster State Park. The center may offer educational programs or exhibits.
Campfire Experience:

Many campsites provide fire rings, allowing you to enjoy a classic camping experience with a campfire. Check park regulations for any fire restrictions and ensure you follow Leave No Trace principles.

Wildlife Watching:

PJ Hoffmaster State Park is likely home to a variety of wildlife. Bring binoculars for birdwatching or keep an eye out for other native species that inhabit the area.
Stargazing:

If camping overnight, take advantage of the opportunity for stargazing. Away from city lights, the park provides a clearer view of the night sky, offering a peaceful and awe-inspiring experience.
Facility Amenities:

Explore any additional amenities provided at the campground, such as restrooms, showers, and picnic areas. Having access to these facilities can enhance your camping comfort.
Reservation Information:

Check the park's reservation policies and availability. PJ Hoffmaster State Park is a popular destination, especially during peak seasons, so securing your campsite in advance is advisable.
Before embarking on your camping trip, review park regulations, camping fees, and any seasonal considerations. Whether you're seeking a quiet retreat or an active outdoor experience, PJ Hoffmaster State Park offers a diverse and picturesque setting for camping enthusiasts.

110.Attend the Polish Heritage Festival.

Attending the Polish Heritage Festival in Grand Rapids promises a celebration of Polish culture, traditions, and a vibrant community spirit. Here's what you can expect during this cultural festival:

Cultural Performances:

Enjoy traditional Polish music, dance, and performances showcasing the rich cultural heritage of Poland. Folk dances, music ensembles, and other artistic expressions often take center stage.
Authentic Cuisine:

Indulge in a variety of authentic Polish dishes and delicacies. From pierogi (dumplings) to kielbasa (sausage), the festival is likely to offer a taste of traditional Polish cuisine.

Travel to Grand Rapids Michigan

Art and Crafts:

Explore booths and exhibits featuring Polish art and crafts. This may include handmade items, traditional costumes, and artwork that reflects the artistic traditions of Poland.
Cultural Exhibits:

Learn about Poland's history, customs, and cultural landmarks through informative exhibits. The festival provides an opportunity to gain insights into the country's heritage.
Traditional Attire:

Many attendees and participants may don traditional Polish attire, adding to the festive atmosphere. It's common to see colorful costumes and garments reflecting different regions of Poland.
Family-Friendly Activities:

The Polish Heritage Festival is likely family-friendly, with activities for children, such as games, crafts, and interactive displays that educate younger generations about Polish culture.
Polka Dancing:

Get ready to dance! Polka music and dancing are integral parts of Polish celebrations. Join in the fun, learn some basic steps, and enjoy the lively atmosphere.
Cultural Workshops:

Participate in workshops or demonstrations that offer hands-on experiences related to Polish traditions. This could include crafts, cooking classes, or language lessons.
Polish Merchandise:

Explore vendor booths offering Polish merchandise, including souvenirs, clothing, and items that celebrate Polish pride. It's an opportunity to bring a piece of Poland home with you.
Community Engagement:

The festival fosters community engagement, bringing together people of Polish descent and those interested in Polish culture. It's a chance to connect with others who share an appreciation for Poland's rich heritage.
Live Entertainment:

Enjoy live music, entertainment, and perhaps even performances by renowned Polish artists. The festival may feature a lineup of musicians and entertainers to keep the celebration lively.
Cultural Presentations:

Attend presentations or talks about Poland's history, traditions, and contemporary culture. Guest speakers may share insights that deepen your understanding of the country.
Before attending, check the festival's schedule, any admission requirements, and specific details about featured performances or activities. The Polish Heritage Festival provides a festive and inclusive environment where attendees can immerse themselves in the warmth of Polish culture and community.

Conclusion

Grand Rapids, Michigan, is a compelling narrative of resilience, growth, and cultural evolution. From its origins as a trading post established by Louis Campau in the early 19th century, the city burgeoned into a vital hub of commerce and industry. The abundant natural resources, particularly the Grand River, played a pivotal role in shaping its destiny.

The 20th century witnessed Grand Rapids transforming into a thriving furniture manufacturing center, earning its moniker as "Furniture City." The city weathered economic shifts and challenges, adapting to new industries and diversifying its economic base. The growth of healthcare, education, and the arts became integral components of its identity.

Grand Rapids' commitment to philanthropy, exemplified by figures like the DeVos and Van Andel families, has had a lasting impact on the community. This philanthropic spirit is reflected in the city's cultural institutions, educational facilities, and public spaces.

Culturally, Grand Rapids has embraced diversity, and its art scene has flourished, epitomized by events like ArtPrize. The city's commitment to sustainability and the environment underscores a forward-thinking mindset that seeks to balance progress with ecological responsibility.

As Grand Rapids steps into the 21st century, its history provides a foundation for continued innovation, inclusivity, and community engagement. The city's story is one of adaptation, collaboration, and a steadfast commitment to enhancing the quality of life for its residents. Grand Rapids stands as a testament to the enduring spirit of a community that has navigated change while preserving the essence of its heritage.

If you enjoyed, please leave a 5-star Amazon Review

To get a free list of people who knows publishing top places to travel all around the world, click this link
https://bit.ly/peoplewhoknowtravel

Travel to Grand Rapids Michigan

References

Resprinter123, CC BY-SA 3.0 <https://creativecommons.org/licenses/by-sa/3.0>, via Wikimedia Commons
https://pixabay.com/photos/spaghetti-pasta-noodles-italian-2931846/

Made in the USA
Monee, IL
15 June 2024

59740495R00105